THE BALANCE OF TERROR

Strategy for the Nuclear Age

THE BALANCE

With a Foreword by Raymond Aron
Translated from the French by Richard Howard

OF TERROR

Strategy for the Nuclear Age

BY PIERRE GALLOIS
French Air Force General (Ret)

1961
HOUGHTON MIFFLIN COMPANY BOSTON
THE RIVERSIDE PRESS CAMBRIDGE

First printing

Au Général Léchères, fidèlement

FOREWORD

My friend General Pierre Gallois has asked me to introduce *The Balance of Terror* to the public. I confess that a foreword seems unnecessary to me: neither author nor book needs a guarantee. But I am delighted to furnish one nevertheless, for I have no reservations about praising this book, a short work but a dense one, which every man with a share of responsibility for the national destiny should read and ponder.

General Gallois is one of those rare soldiers, those rare men, who have a warm heart and a cool head, who prefer wisdom to popularity, who put their trust in facts and reason and challenge traditional doctrines. Convinced that the so-called massive-destruction weapons, both atomic and thermonuclear, have opened a new era in the history of war and therefore of society, he follows his analysis to its logical conclusion, applying to a situation created by mutual capacity for destruction all the resources of a mind both logical and subtle.

For logic and subtlety are equally essential to the understanding of today's strategy, and tomorrow's: logic to determine what behavior is the rational consequence of the explosive power of nuclear weapons, subtlety to anticipate the probable conduct of nations in a universe where a misunderstanding or an error in calculation would provoke an unparalleled castastrophe.

At the present time, two states possess thermonuclear weapons and carrying vehicles of such a nature that in case of a conflict each would be in a position to inflict on the other damage out of all proportion to the possible advantages of victory. Furthermore, even if one state were to make a surprise attack on the other's means of reprisal, the side attacked would have enough bombs, planes or missiles left over to inflict enormous devastation on the aggressor's cities. The immediate reaction of well-intentioned pacifists to this balance of terror is to insist on "general disarmament and periodic check." And M. Jules Moch denounces "the madness of men." But are men really mad?

As a matter of fact, it is impossible to guarantee the elimination of bomb stockpiles. Even if statesmen did not suspect each other of the worst, the suppression of massive-destruction weapons would probably be impossible. In the world's present state, these weapons make highly unlikely the very war pacifists so rightly detest. Nations have always waged war against each other: what would stop them from doing so in the twentieth century, once they no longer feared the atom's demoniacal power? Indeed the worst solution, the one that would create the greatest risk, would be to "outlaw" atomic weapons, spreading the illusion that only conventional weapons would be used in a war among the major powers. Once engaged in the struggle, every major power would hasten to produce the explosives allegedly outlawed. Humanity's only chance, in the present phase, is to maintain peace by the anguish which the mere mention of thermonuclear war inspires. Peace the scion of war? It would not be the first nor the worst of Reason's ruses.

Starting from this premise, not arbitrarily advanced but solidly grounded in reason, General Gallois introduces us to the strange world of atomic strategy. And a strange strategy too, based on the threat of a war no one wants to fight, an absurd, monstrous war. Is it possible to adopt a strategy which brandishes the threat of universal suicide?

General Gallois attempts a rational formulation of the diplomacy of dissuasion — that diplomacy which uses thermonuclear "terrorism" to dissuade a possible aggressor from certain undertakings. This rational formulation is articulated around principles of proportionality: a thermonuclear threat will be taken seriously by the threatened power only to the degree that the stake of the conflict seems in proportion to the consequences the threat's execution would produce. But perhaps we credit these hypothetical appraisals with excessive rigor. No stake is proportional to thermonuclear suicide. If the threat functions, in spite of everything, it is because once it creates the shadow of a doubt it is effective. The threat, one might say, is equal to the product of the likelihood of its execution by the consequences which this execution would produce. If the likelihood exists at all, then strategy can be used and can succeed.

General Gallois presents and solves two other problems which have preoccupied experts for years. Will thermonuclear weapons help prevent any war, or prevent a major war and favor limited war? Heretofore most experts have

advocated the second alternative. The more monstrous the
threat, the less often it can be wielded, and with total war
hypothetically outlawed, limited conflicts — limited in relation to the field of battle as well as to the weapons employed — remain possible. General Gallois tends to favor
the first alternative, at least in cases where major powers are
involved. The argument he advances is that of "escalation." Today the major powers possess a continuous series
of atomic weapons, the smallest of which have an explosive
power comparable to that of the TNT bombs of World
War II (calculated in units of tons of TNT), and the largest an explosive power a thousand times greater than that
of the bomb dropped on Hiroshima (calculated in millions
of tons of TNT). At the time of the Korean war, there was
a great disparity between the strongest classical weapon
and the weakest atomic weapon. This disparity no longer
exists. Lacking a solution of continuity, the distinction between classical weapons and atomic weapons tends to disappear, thereby obliging the major powers to avoid limited
wars because they could no longer be certain of avoiding
their extension. Let us hope that General Gallois is right,
and that if the H-bombs forbid an all-out war, the "escalator" principle will prevent limited ones.

The second problem, of particular interest to us as
Frenchmen, is that of the fourth atomic power (or the fifth,
the sixth, etc.). The overwhelming majority of world
opinion favors "closing" the atomic club. General Gallois
takes the contrary view, which I believe to be well founded.
The thermonuclear threat will be less and less plausible if
it fails to protect the very state that brandishes it. Ultimately, no state could protect another from the thermonuclear threat, since the possible aggressor would no longer

take such a threat seriously in behalf of a protégé. Let us accept this reasoning, though it is far from being incontestable: as in the case of "escalation," we are dealing with a psychological hypothesis. The second stage of the theory is the assertion that a small atomic force (a few dozen bombs and carrying vehicles) has a defensive value. As a matter of fact, the state possessing such a force would itself be of medium size: threatening the aggressor with a small atomic attack (that is, with the equivalent of a few Hiroshimas), it still makes aggression unreasonable: why should the Soviet Union destroy France if, in retaliation, several A-bombs would be dropped on Leningrad and Moscow? The argument is valid if we suppose the small atomic force safe from surprise attack and the medium-size state capable of convincing the major powers that under certain conditions it would accept annihilation rather than surrender.

If the logic of this argument were to prevail, humanity would move toward an increasingly numerous atom club. Yet if too many states possess such weapons, the hypothesis on which the preceding arguments are based — that is, the rationality of diplomatic behavior — would grow less and less certain. Therefore it seems to me that the solution should be sought in the direction of what is called a double check. Atomic weapons would not be limited to the major powers alone, stockpiled only on the territory of the protecting nation, but the distribution of atomic weapons throughout the NATO nations would be effected in such a way that none could use these weapons offensively and all could use them for their own defense. The present double-check formula would need only one security clause: if one of the member nations were exclusively and immediately exposed to the pressure of a major power, it would obtain free use of the weapons of dissuasion.

I have said enough to show the reader the interest of General Gallois' book. This aviator who spends his spare time covering the walls of his house with frescoes is, as Tocqueville said of the French nation, "apt in everything but excelling only in war." Above all he excels in the art of *thinking war*. In our time, the art of war is identified with the art of preventing war. And how prevent war if not by inciting statesmen to rational behavior, utilizing the horror which the mere mention of the Apocalypse inspires? Perhaps General Gallois puts too much faith in the rationality of statesmen. *Felix culpa,* if by reading his book the latter become what this intellectual, long disguised as a soldier, believes they will be.

RAYMOND ARON

CONTENTS

THE BALANCE OF TERROR

Strategy for the Nuclear Age

INTRODUCTION

"If the Russians, the Americans and the British simultaneously destroyed their nuclear missiles on neutral terrain, if they then collected the fissionable material and handed it over to an international organization pledged to use it for peaceful purposes, the present insecurity would be brought to an end." This, in substance, is the assertion of Mr. Thomas F. Murray, former member of the United States Atomic Energy Commission.

"The thermonuclear bomb is a diabolical invention," wrote Professor Max Born. A few months after this declaration by the father of modern physics, eighteen German physicists, including four Nobel Prize-winners, sent an appeal to their government and their fellow citizens, asking that atomic weapons be banned forever.

During the summer of 1959, Hugh Gaitskell, condemning the policy his own party had hitherto pursued, demanded that Great Britain destroy its stockpile of nuclear weapons and take the initiative in grouping all nations of good will into a "club" of non-atom countries which would leave the two Great Powers a monopoly of the new

weapons. The approaching election justified this attitude.
A year earlier, seeking a good electoral platform, the Liberal party had already taken a similar stand. The proposition had three advantages: it pleased a public opinion
terrified by the perils of radioactivity; it limited the dissemination of atomic weapons which appeared so dangerous
to all governments; and it condemned the new British defense policy as defined by the White Paper of 1957 and
opposed by almost the entire British armament industry, deprived for almost two years of its previous subsidies.
It must be remembered that in the days of TNT, a nation's military power was measured not by the size of its
explosives stockpile, but only by the number of explosive-
bearing "vehicles" it had in readiness, and "vehicle"
means here the assault tank, the plane or the cruiser, as
well as the infantryman carrying a rifle or machine gun.
Executing combat operations consisted of collecting at the
right place the maximum number of "carrying vehicles"
— soldiers, tanks, planes, etc. — each with a limited destructive power, but whose number furnished power and,
in most cases of numerical superiority, victory as well.
Atomic explosives have altered this notion which is as old
as the art of war itself. The goal remains the same — to
outstrip the adversary's destructive power — but the
means are different. Because of the new explosive, the accumulation of men and materiel is no longer necessary.
To pursue a policy of dissuasion based on nuclear strength
would therefore revolutionize the existing organization
of planning and production. This transformation, like the
contraction of the armament industries which occurred
after the publication of the White Paper of 1957 and
1958, did not win complete support.

Beyond the Rhine, the world of politics followed the lead of the world of science. It was Doctor Jaeger, Vice-President of the Bundestag, chairman of the Assembly's military committee and an influential member of the government party, who opposed a possible dissemination of long-range nuclear weapons in Germany. "The Bundeswehr must be only a defensive force," declared the chairman of the military committee, apparently unaware that a defense policy based on defensive weapons alone would now — as for a long time past — be meaningless. An "appeal to oppose atomic death," signed by some forty leaders in the world of politics, science, and the arts, was made to the German people. It demanded the outlawing of nuclear weapons in Germany and the condemnation of "an armament policy which threatened the nation's very existence . . ." [1]

Even before the NATO session of December 1957, Herr Strauss, Federal Minister of Defense, had been obliged to emphasize the fact that the German government would limit itself to conventional armaments, to the exclusion of "atomic, bacteriological, and chemical weapons . . ." And soon afterward Herr von Brentano, the Federal Republic's Foreign Affairs Minister, declared that "there

[1] To the appeal of the eighteen German physicists asking that massive-destruction weapons be permanently banned, Chancellor Adenauer had coolly replied that the introduction of atomic weapons into the arsenal of the German armies' new forces was a matter of general policy and consequently that the eighteen scientists were not competent to discuss it. Fritz Heine, chief of the Social Democratic party's press service, immediately asserted that the Chancellor's answer was "the greatest insult made to the German physicists by a politician who has neither experience nor knowledge in the realm of science, particularly in nuclear physics." As a matter of fact, Heine was exploiting for political purposes a perfectly well-founded remark by the head of the German government, the problem being a political one and not of a scientific nature.

could be no question of the installation in Germany of launching sites for ballistic missiles at the present time." In France, too, opposition to the new weapons was first evidenced in scientific circles. In October 1954, M. Louis Leprince-Ringuet wrote in *La Croix:* "On no account, therefore, must we devote our scientists, our money, our research to the manufacture of atomic bombs." The following year, speaking to a specifically Christian audience, Monsieur André Piettre, professor at the Faculté de Droit in Paris, wrote: "Have we the right to annihilate humanity in order to save Christendom? For this, ultimately, is the fundamental problem . . ." More recently, the French Federation Against Atomic Weapons issued its own appeal, signed by some 350 famous names and asking the country to relinquish "all nuclear tests" and to "support the proposal of the International Red Cross, which would lead to the banning of nuclear weapons."

The preparations for the first French atomic explosion mobilized the new weapon's adversaries. The National Synod of the Church of France asked the French government to devote nuclear research to exclusively peaceful applications. "Personally," Pastor Westphal declared, "I feel that the greatness of France should manifest itself in other realms than that of nuclear experiments." And the Methodist Pastor Peter Decadu, a member of the Executive Committee of the World Council of Churches, asked the Committee to lodge a protest with the French Government against the projected tests in the Sahara . . .

In November 1959, after visiting a Russian factory annually manufacturing some 250 missiles with thermonuclear warheads, Mr. Khrushchev declared: "We're ready to throw all this to the bottom of the sea to insure world peace. Far from wanting war, we do not even want the means to make war." The Soviet Chief of State was forgetting that once the world is rid of atomic and thermonuclear weapons, the Soviets would still retain the numerical advantage, at least in relation to the West.

This imbalance in the instruments of power was probably not apparent to Mr. George Kennan, former United States Ambassador to Moscow, when he said, in substance, on the BBC: "It is nonsense to base one's security on a weapon which, employed in a war, would mean suicide for both sides. The maintenance of atomic armament would be comprehensible only if we considered ourselves inferior in the realm of conventional weapons . . ." Which is obviously the case and singularly weakens the effect of Mr. Kennan's anti-atomic appeal.

Partisans of the position we have just reviewed were inspired by a feeling of natural generosity or by fear. And fear in this case is the result of a normal intellectual process: the association of the new weapon's destructive effects with the memory of yesterday's conflicts. Since Hiroshima, all humanity, enlightened by its intellectuals, has seen in the phenomena of atomic fission and fusion only a formidable development of destructive power. That there should be a discontinuity in the consequences as in the technical fact, that yesterday's reasoning should no longer apply today, and that it is no longer feasible to conduct classical military operations with nuclear weapons — this tremendous gap between the era of conventional weapons and the atomic age is apparent to very few.

In short, according to all these opponents of the atom, we must return at all costs, and as fast as possible, to the age of trinitrotoluene.

Was that age so remarkable that we should be homesick for it now? Was it humanity's golden age?

In Europe, the period we can properly call the age of TNT had the Battle of Crécy, in 1346, as its first landmark. Gunpowder's hegemony and the age itself came to an end at Hiroshima in 1945, when atomic explosives were added to the arsenal of classical chemical explosives. The six centuries between are stigmatized by an uninterrupted series of wars. Professor Quincy Wright observes that between 1482 and 1941, that is, between the Treaty of Arras which established the success of Louis XI's efforts and, in fact, the end of feudalism, and the United States' entry into World War II, some 278 wars can be listed, the term here indicating armed confrontations of at least 50,000 combatants, or else conflicts entailing a state of war in the juridical sense of the word. This period coincides, to a few years, with the age of TNT. The inventory of the devastation wrought during these 459 years of permanent conflict is grim enough so that we need not try to reproduce their conditions again. It is difficult to see humanity's advantage in reverting to an age characterized by so much human and material destruction.

Ever since men first confronted each other with side arms or gunpowder, and until Hiroshima, the "quantity of destruction" they could inflict was fractional, limited, finite. To some extent there could be an acceptable relation between the value of the conflict's object and the sacrifices made in order to seize or defend it. One could set off on a campaign with a light heart, as was the case until almost the end of the nineteenth century; one might even conceive of fighting to protect property or defend ideas whose security deserved the sacrifice of hundreds of thousands of human lives and the annihilation of important material resources, as was still the case in the first half of the twentieth century. This is no longer true; the devastation has assumed such dimensions that the conflict's very purpose would disappear with it.

Today, nuclear armament poses the classical problem of war in an entirely new way:

1. There is no longer any common measure between the conflict's purpose and the risk run in attacking by force. Yesterday, the fractionalization of destructive power permitted an adaptation to the causes and the nature of the dispute. War could sometimes be an intelligent operation. Yesterday, one began a campaign once a fly-swatter had landed on the nose of the French Consul in Algiers or upon reading a garbled dispatch.

Today, this is no longer the case. Once the process has begun, the risk is exorbitant, the retribution immediate, the recourse to force senseless. When two nations are armed with nuclear weapons, even if they are unequally armed, the status quo is unavoidable. The aggressor nation, even if it were stronger, would in fact risk losing in a few hours the advantage of all its past efforts: transformed into a desert, it would be thrown several decades or even centuries behind the rest. This nation — and those of its inhabitants who had escaped death, either immediate or by radiation poisoning — would have irremediably lost the economic and political race, and the very objects of its ambition would be swept from the face of the earth.

When Mao Tse-tung suggests that his country is not afraid of the nuclear threat, that it could lose 300 million inhabitants and thereby triumph over an adversary not possessing such enormous human reserves, he is wrong. It happens that there are no other technical and industrial civilizations than those based on urban agglomerations — on cities. The modernization of China, too, presupposes the development of urban life. Nuclear weapons have not only radiation effects, they also have mechanical effects — shock and heat — which are not selective. One cannot attack a great nation, destroy 300 million of its inhabitants, and at the same time leave the necessary means of modern life intact for the survivors. If China lost 300 million inhabitants, she would be hurled back into the vacuum from which Mao Tse-tung is, in fact, trying to extricate her. Even Peking cannot gamble on a war, if that war is a nuclear one: such speculation would be as childish as it was stupid.

In every case, whatever the nations involved, devastation could reach such proportions that a nation's very existence would have to be threatened before it would consider using its atomic arsenal. For the rest, one must accept the notion of a *fait accompli*. If Soviet pursuit planes force down an American plane or if American artillery opens fire on a Soviet plane, nothing happens. Nothing happens — except diplomatic protests and demands for indemnities — because nothing can happen. And even if transport planes were forced down, even if civilian passengers were the victims of a pursuit pilot's nervous trigger finger or of hostile antiaircraft batteries, nothing would happen. The devastation would so obviously be out of all proportion to the misdemeanor that such a war is unthinkable. Clearly, if nuclear weapons had not existed, the face of the world since 1945 would have been changed and would have been changed by force.

2. Under certain conditions, a new form of equality can

be established among nations. In questions of security and defense, there can no longer be strong nations and weak nations — at least in facing certain dangers.

The notion seems paradoxical enough to require some justification. Let us take the case of Denmark.

In 1864 and 1865, this country had not been able to resist Prussian and Austrian aggression. It was invaded in 1940 by the troops of the Third Reich. Unfortunately situated geographically, rich, civilized, peace-loving, with few human and material means of defense at its command, Denmark virtually invites invasion. Today, facing overwhelming Soviet superiority, it owes its independence only to the collective defense system to which it belongs. But if, tomorrow, Denmark found itself alone, it would undoubtedly be doomed as it was in 1864 and 1940. It was out of the question, in those days, for a country Denmark's size to command conventional forces adequate to defend its neutrality. In the age of the new weapons, however, Denmark could still base its security on the possession of a few nuclear-warhead missiles, whether these weapons were purely national or, as is more likely, if they were placed under the double control of Denmark and the guarantor nation. If, for instance, the Danish government possessed several missile-launching submarines, it would have an effective dissuasion force, because the latter would be difficult to destroy preventively and because the destructive power they represented would greatly exceed the advantage the aggressor might derive from a subjugated Denmark. Who would dare attack this small country, if, in order to depose its government and invade its territory, the aggressor would have to run the risk, in return, of seeing a dozen of his own major urban cen-

ters destroyed? Would access to the North Sea and control
of the Straits be worth such devastation? Of course, confronted with an ultimatum accompanied by threats of
atomic dissuasion, or even with the invasion of its territory
by forces greatly superior in number, the Danish government would probably surrender rather than launch its
missiles and subsequently suffer the effects of the aggressor's retaliation. But what if it did not surrender? What
if it used its missiles? The aggressor would prove his vulnerability to a small state's power. He would have to bind
up his wounds while the rival great nations continued the
race toward prosperity. But above all, the aggressor
would be facing a dilemma: if he did not brutally retaliate against the Danish reaction, he would lose face and
prove the value of the policy of nuclear decentralization;
yet if the aggressor made the Danes pay dearly for their
national impulse, the horror his retaliation inspired
would risk turning the rest of the world against him.

Obviously the likelihood of a Danish nuclear reaction is
slight, but what counts is that this slight likelihood is com-
pensated for by an enormous destructive power, certainly
a destructive power superior to the relatively limited
value Denmark represents. By reacting in this way to an
attack, Denmark would doubtless be condemning itself
to destruction and committing a kind of national suicide. It is quite likely that it would abjure such a reprisal,
preferring servitude to annihilation. Yet who would
have the audacity to gamble on a government's weakness,
if in case of an error in anticipating its conduct, the aggressor's losses were so terrible, and so greatly out of
proportion with the conflict's goal? Tomorrow, the combination of submarine and ballistic missiles can satisfy the

requirements of the Danish dissuasion policy. Thereafter some other technical formula will no doubt be employed, but a certain leveling principle among small nations and large abides.

3. Because new weapons, based on the principle of atomic fission but of lower power, are beginning to figure in the panoplies of the two Great Powers, the concept of dissuasion will henceforth be applied not only to the defense of states of major importance but also to secondary conflicts. Because destructive power by "firing unit" now ranges from grenade to thermonuclear bomb without a real solution of continuity between conventional explosives and atomic explosives, we can anticipate a tremendous strategic and political upheaval.

Only ten years ago, at the start of the Korean war, there existed an enormous difference between the most powerful TNT weapons and the least powerful American atomic weapons normally usable at the time. This difference was of a psychological nature, of course, but also of a mechanical order; the first of these weapons destroyed several hundred square yards of terrain, whereas the second destroyed everything in an area of twelve to fifteen thousand square yards. It was apparent the world over that the stake of the Korean conflict was not in proportion to a new Hiroshima. Because of the moral constraint the United States then imposed upon itself — and also because of the insistence of the French and British governments — the conflict lasted years and tens of thousands of young Americans were sacrificed, Washington waging 12,000 kilometers from its bases a costly war that only the threat of using atomic weapons might have stopped. But the memory of Hiroshima was still fresh, and America,

taking its allies' advice, preferred to oppose the Chinese
masses with its divisions and its aerial and naval squadrons.

Because the physicists are continually reducing the destructive power of atomic explosions, this period is now
past. If there were a conflict tomorrow between those nations possessing a complete atomic panoply, the danger
would be that, rather than surrender, each belligerent
would successively resort to weapons of greater and
greater power, crossing the atomic threshold all the more
easily the closer it lies to conventional weapons. This
would constitute the principle of "escalation," each side using increasingly powerful weapons against the other and
the damage mutually endured quickly exceeding in extent the value of the conflict's initial purpose. Since neither side is unaware of the dangers in this rising scale of
destructive powers, and since each side realizes, before beginning, the absurdity of a trial by force that would either
lead to mutual destruction or oblige one side to surrender
in time — but which? — it is clear that other procedures
than direct armed attack must be employed. This is why
the *coup d'état,* the palace revolution, and subversion are
henceforth to be substituted for the old open hostilities.
If the new explosive cannot impose total peace, at least it
limits the intensity of the conflict and condemns pitched
battle as it condemns yesterday's wars of position and
movement.

4. By combining thermonuclear explosives with long-
range ballistic missiles, technologists have created a
weapon against which, today, there is no defense. It appears that whoever uses it first must triumph and that
this weapon gives the aggressor an enormous advantage.

As a matter of fact, if both sides possess such weapons — even in unequal numbers — this need not be the case. If he wishes to avoid suffering their terrible effects himself, the assailant must first destroy his victim's reprisal missiles before they are launched against his own territory. In short, he must execute a successful counterbattery and annihilate his enemy's missiles in their launching silos. But this counterbattery can be made impossible; if the missiles the aggressor must destroy are protected underground or if they are made mobile and their movements concealed from the potential aggressor, the latter cannot prepare himself against retaliation. Therefore, contrary to what is usually supposed, the appearance of ballistic missiles with thermonuclear warheads does not facilitate aggression, but on the contrary, given certain precautions, makes it virtually impracticable.

Of course, these precautions will be increasingly complex and increasingly costly, but they must condemn taking the initiative in matters of force. There is no analogous situation to be found in history. Doubtless for the first time, opposing sides, their arsenals full, cannot come to grips with each other. If one side abjures the necessary efforts of preparation and is technologically outstripped, the other triumphs. But if the technological race continues at the same rate on both sides, the status quo is obligatory, firm, and immutable.

For all these reasons, before insisting on the suppression of nuclear armament, the governments of the Western democracies would do better to reflect. Perhaps it is wiser to prepare for an atomic war that cannot occur, thereby maintaining a state of equilibrium among the unequal forces throughout the world, than to accumulate the weapons of a conflict which would be possible because it would be waged by purely conventional means.

Is the nuclear phenomenon revolutionary enough to outdate war at last? If there were a respite, could the world utilize the time to remedy its inequalities, so that the very causes of international conflict would gradually disappear? The pages that follow have a more modest goal than to answer such questions: their purpose is to outline the metamorphoses in armament techniques and to draw their military and political consequences.

I POWDER WITHOUT FIRE

In less than fifteen years a new and terrible arsenal has been created. Almost every month, one side or the other adds new weapons to its panoply, and if these weapons were to be used, it would be under conditions quite different from those which memory or history record. Since Hiroshima, specialists have unceasingly studied the most likely form of a conflict during which the entire range of these new techniques would be utilized. Their recommendations have resulted in an organization, an armament and a "posture" of the armed forces concerned, which seems to them most likely to discourage aggression and, should this first mission fail, to direct the ensuing combat operations to a victorious conclusion.[1]

A number of new strategic concepts, acknowledged by the general staffs and specialists of virtually all the major powers, are responsible for these attempts to adapt clas-

[1] Each side has its own notion of what such victorious combat operations might be. But no one can know the precise extent of the disaster — on both sides — which would result from the execution of nuclear operations.

sical military doctrine to the probable nature of a nuclear war.

As long as gunpowder was used, destructive power was based on the sum and even on the accumulation, in as large proportions as possible, of means of transporting and "applying" gunfire. Since these "carrying vehicles" [1] were individually furnished with only a slight destructive power, their number had to be multiplied. And the side outnumbering the other had at least a material superiority.

Wars were therefore preceded by a rearmament period during which the industries involved constructed these carrying vehicles and accumulated stockpiles. Such an effort could not pass unobserved. The country threatened by these preparations was quite aware of the risks it ran by remaining idle. Possessing the material and moral means, it could face the danger and muster the forces that would permit it either to negotiate on a basis of equality or to enter the conflict and at least make its defeat a costly one. Mobilization preceded battle, and both sides had time enough to shift from a state of armed peace to a state of war.

Today, the phases in this gradual evolution from peace to war have been abolished. By using only a minor share — numerically speaking — of the armed forces they maintain in peacetime, the United States and the U.S.S.R. could in a few hours or a few days inflict mutual damage severe enough to bring all organized combat to a halt. Consequently a surprise attack would be essen-

1 The term must be understood to include the infantryman and his rifle, the tank and its cannon, the plane and its machine gun or its bombs, the submarine and its torpedoes, and lastly the ballistic missile carrying its explosive charge thousands of kilometers.

tial, in which preparations could be limited enough so that only vague hints could be detected — particularly on the Russian side, because of the hermetic nature of the Soviet territory; the actual alarm would be given only with the appearance on American radar screens of echoes corresponding to enemy planes or missiles. The fact that the aggressor can now take the offensive without giving the alarm changes everything: industrial mobilization becomes impossible; reserves can play a role only on the spot, in civil or passive defense; there is no time to muster the nation's human resources and hurl them into battle; a nation's institutions, its administrative machinery, even its military command can no longer *adjust to* a state of war — it is at war from the start. Active air defense has lost its importance: if it were really caught off guard, it would not attain a tenth of the effectiveness of the aggressor nation's already alerted defense system. A land army could be destroyed before it was ever engaged and naval forces annihilated at anchor. . . . Only a professional army in a state of permanent alert, as ready to intervene as the aggressor's forces on the day of attack, is of any value in dealing with this form of sudden warfare.

If surprise aggression is henceforth technically possible, the "quantity of destruction" applicable in a very brief period would be of such extent that the "organized" phase of the war would be of brief duration. An enemy could probably devastate the United States in an hour or two by launching the 263 thermonuclear missiles whose destructive effects have been studied by a group of American experts investigating the consequences of an attack on United States territory. Perhaps in less than two hours, since the missiles take only thirty minutes to complete their enormous trajectory and land 8000 kilometers from their launching sites.

The classical notion of a slow erosion, each of the belligerents wearing away the other's potential or sapping its combat morale, yields to a single surprise attack from which a whole nation would not recover. Formerly a function of time, since it applied to a conflict of several years' duration, destructive energy has now become independent of it.

This tremendous contraction of the period of confrontation also revolutionizes the conflict's conditions. Once such a war is begun, it is too late to modify its procedure and its forms. It is no longer possible to mobilize new military classes, conclude new alliances or speculate on a scientific discovery capable of affecting the course of events. There is no time. The exchange of attacks — if there were an exchange — would be brief. Planning is not impossible, nor is the estimate of mutually suffered material damages, but too many factors intervene to permit measures to be taken against the consequences of the initial operation.

A country — or a coalition — pursuing a strictly defensive policy has the double disadvantage of being liable to surprise attack and of being able to retaliate only after it has "absorbed" the first assault. And since the first assault may be decisive, this country has no choice but to dissuade its adversary from resorting to force by proving that a first assault could not destroy its own reprisal forces, and that the aggressor would consequently have to suffer their effects.

One must add to the factors of surprise and the contraction of the period of confrontation a new concept that is also peculiar to thermonuclear war — the concept of risk.

Though the last two World Wars were certainly wars of extermination, they were not intended as such when the first battles began. A decision was anticipated on the basis of a rapid conflict. But each side also knew that it had a certain recuperative power which it could draw on during the course of the struggle. Each belligerent planned to adapt itself to its adversary's actions, hoping to gain victory by mobilizing new resources and utilizing them more astutely. There was a risk, but it was limited by two factors: in case of defeat, punitive sanction did not mean annihilation of the loser; also, time allowed for many variations in status, including a demand for an armistice if conditions were too unfavorable. This too has changed. On the one hand, in case of the initial assault's failure, the aggressor nation must expect — during the minutes that follow its attack — to suffer reprisals that would hurl it ten centuries into the past; and on the other, there would be no time for a nation to adapt itself to the adversary's forces and strategy. It would have to endure their crushing effects immediately. The fact that the risk is henceforth incommensurable with what it was in the days of "conventional" war has significant military and political consequences as well. If nations were ever to resort to thermonuclear weapons, the stake of the conflict would automatically become a capital one. The prospects of an exchange of atomic attacks are grim enough for it to be envisaged only as a last resort, when the very life of the nation engaged is at stake, and even then . . .

Nor can we any longer measure the military superiority of one nation over another in the same way. Yesterday, a

nation with a hundred divisions could normally expect to
beat a nation that had only sixty, and the former could
run the risk of attacking the latter. But if today we char-
acterize the power of nation A by assigning it five hundred
nuclear units[1] and the power of nation B by assigning it
three hundred similar nuclear units, nation A could nevertheless not take the risk of attacking nation B. To do
so, the quantitative and qualitative margin of superiority
would have to be large enough for the aggressor to be certain either that there would be no reprisal or else that
this reprisal would be "absorbable." In such a case, uncertainty is worth enormous "quantities of destruction."
Numerical superiority is no longer decisive, at least to a
certain degree. Though stronger than the nation it wishes
to attack, the aggressor would still be paralyzed. If Western public opinion had a clearer notion of this new by-
product — ultimately a reassuring one — of the thermonuclear age, it would better understand the rules of the
game being played by American and Soviet diplomacy.

Each member of NATO may wonder if, in the view of
the Allied group, its value corresponds to the risks that
group would have to take in order to defend it, and may
ask itself the following question: what would happen if an
incident of major importance to the independence or
security of one member nation were considered minor by
the guarantor atomic powers and by the other member
nations? For this estimate of the vital or minor character
of a threat against one of the Allies can no longer be
made, save as a function of a new criterion: the extent
of the risk that must be run in its defense. But the same

1 *Nuclear unit* refers here to the combination of an atomic charge and the
appropriate carrying vehicle.

reasoning is followed by the other side: the risks to be run are weighed on the other side of the iron curtain too, and since it is this side that must take the initiative — not endure it — the risk with regard to the same objective would appear even greater.

Surprise, contraction of the extermination phase, and exorbitant risk can neither replace nor be added to the celebrated principles of war when a nation contemplates using megatons. It is a question, at best, of the rules of action with which one must deal.

What form would a so-called generalized conflict take — that is, a conflict during which the United States and the Soviet Union would confront each other directly? The probability of such a confrontation is extremely slight, but it is only by examining its possible development that we realize *why* it is virtually impossible.

If they are not yet all accounted for, the means of Soviet expansion are many and contradictory. Before writing President Eisenhower that he "hoped for an immediate change in international relations," Khrushchev had often spoken words of a different nature. "We'll bury you all!" he once remarked to both the capitalist world and the United States. At the end of June 1959, this was how he described the situation in Berlin and Formosa to Mr. Averell Harriman: "If you want war, you'll get it; our missiles will be launched automatically . . . The Soviet Union strongly supports China's claims to Formosa, and if it comes to a show of force, the Soviets will make their contribution."

During the Suez crisis, when Khrushchev referred indirectly to the atomization of Paris and London, did he have instruments for such a move at his disposal, even if he had no intention of using them? Or was the Soviet leader merely gambling on the ignorance of Western public opinion which echoes like a gong at almost every nod from the Kremlin, imposing negotiation — even conciliation at any price — upon governments that are hesitant and chiefly concerned to express public feeling, even when it is based on purely emotional factors?

At the end of June 1960 — that is, after the failure of the Summit Conference — Khrushchev returned to the theme of Communism's invincible force that would conquer the world without recourse to war. In Bucharest, at the Congress of the Rumanian Workers' Party, he declared: "We Communists know that our cause will win . . . I could not say: let us make war, half the world will die, the other half survive . . . If I said such a thing, you could put me in a strait jacket. We shall be smarter than that. We shall make the imperialists wriggle like fish frying in oil, and this without any armed conflict." Khrushchev's variations on the theme of war and peace tend further in the direction of forced peace than toward inevitable war. Ten years earlier, Stalin had evidently not grasped the inflexible logic of the atomic era. He probably had only a vague conception of the new explosives' significance in military terms. As we shall see below, the experts surrounding him were no better informed. After the victory over the Third Reich, no Russian could admit that a force as powerful as the Red Army could be defeated by a few bombs, even bombs of unprecedented power. Of course it was widely known that the American atomic stockpile was then limited to projectiles in the kiloton range and that the planes carrying them were not invulnerable. So that despite his brutality and his capacity for simplification, Stalin was taking only reasonable risks in carrying out his policy of expansion by force or by threat of force. No doubt he speculated vaguely on the new weapons' unsuitability to the forms of conflict he was provoking. Either they were all-powerful, and the *casus belli* he was creating — in Korea, for instance — failed to correspond to their nature; or else there were not enough of them, and not enough was known about them, to determine the consequences of their use, and Washington would not dare put itself in the position of having to employ them in large quantities.

From 1945 to 1953 or 1954, a period characterized by the American atomic monopoly, Soviet expansion in Europe was limited only by United States negotiation and, later, by the North Atlantic treaty. Hitherto everything had occurred as though Moscow deliberately ignored American military possibilities, while Washington took no further account of the decisive nature of the means the West then possessed to oblige the Communist menace to withdraw. Each side had been the dupe of the atom: the Soviets, in their ignorance, not fearing it; and the Americans not realizing the advantage their monopoly might have given them.

As for the Russian military experts, they have written what they thought of the new weapons. Soviet military doctrine is defined by many texts, almost all of which are characterized by the contradiction between Leninist notions of war and the new weapons of massive destruction. And it cannot be easy, in the U.S.S.R., to act in any official capacity against the prevailing dogma. In 1955, Major General Pokrovsky, the Soviet general staff expert on nu-

clear weapons and missiles, wrote: "Atomic and thermonuclear weapons, in their present state of development,
merely add to the firing power of other more conventional forms of armament."

And for his part General Krasilnikov said of nuclear
war that "it would not involve the reduction of the number of combatants. On the contrary, it would logically impose their numerical increase . . ." Still more formally,
the same General Pokrovsky listed today's techniques and
yesterday's, concluding with the permanence of traditional military concepts: "In war, the only correct method
of using the various military techniques is that of Soviet
military science, which shows that all forms of armament
and technique must be used conjointly, during well-
planned combined operations. Soviet military science
teaches that the only way of winning a war today is to
conduct combined operations using all weapons and services in a perfectly coherent way."

In the thermonuclear age, when Khrushchev so often
brandishes the threat of general atomic destruction, this
ultraclassical conception of the armed forces' role would
be surprising if we did not take into consideration the
ends and means of Soviet policy. On the other hand, the
West, after taking stock of its resources, has realized that
to offset the East's enormous demographic power, it must
have recourse to the new weapons. This concept has
proved valid for the defense of certain important goals,
inadequate for others. Naturally the monovalence of
Western military possibilities has reinforced the value of
the polyvalence of Soviet forces. Nuclear armament holds
— and claims to hold — only one battlement of the Western fortress, while the rest endure the assaults of a varied

force with numerous resources. Hence, when in November 1957 Defense Minister Malinovsky, speaking before the young officers of the Russian Military Academy, endorsed notions that seemed largely outdated, this did not mean that the potentialities of the new nuclear strategy had not been grasped on the other side of the Iron Curtain.

But the discovery is relatively recent, dating back to 1954 and 1955. It appears, in this area, that second-hand knowledge is inadequate, and it was undoubtedly necessary for many Soviet generals to observe atomic tests in order for them to glimpse the vulnerability of masses of combatants, the weaknesses of numerical strategy, and even the considerable risk of relying on a show of force. We can discern the same development of such ideas in China, where the "tack" toward atomic strategy is still to be taken. When at the end of July 1958, Khrushchev met with Mao Tse-tung, they undoubtedly determined to sound out American intentions with regard to Quemoy and Matsu, and to see if the Pentagon would go so far as to use the new low-power atomic weapons. It was on the advice of the Soviet leader that the decision not to run excessive risks was made. On the other hand, in one of the last statements (October 1959) of the Chinese Minister of Defense, Marshal Lin Piao, there is nothing which reveals any particular understanding of the nuclear problem, and it is undoubtedly to this state of mind that we must attribute the Sino-Russian dispute as to the conditions of victory within the Marxist-Leninist camp.

By his repeated declarations and his use of the threat of nuclear war, Khrushchev indicates that he has clearly grasped the possibilities and also the limitations of the ballistic and thermonuclear arsenal which the Soviets have accumulated. There is a great difference between making and materializing such threats, and the Soviet command now knows the extent of the task which would face it — and the enormity of the risks to be run — should it be necessary to take action.

If as a general staff exercise, for instance, the devastation of a large part of the American territory were made a study project, the procedure adopted would be more or less as follows: first the Soviet government would have to evaluate the risk it would be willing to run in order to clear — brutally but surely — the road to world hegemony. This risk, translated into "quantities of destruction," would have to be compared with the possibilities of American reprisal, supposing, at the worst, that the latter could be launched effectively.

During the first months of hostilities of World War II, the U.S.S.R. lost four million combatants. The losses it suffered in expelling and finally defeating the invader have been estimated[1] at some twenty million human lives; it has also been said that the agrarian reforms caused drastic changes in the Soviet demography. Bearing these figures in mind, American specialists say it is not unreasonable to suppose that under certain circumstances the U.S.S.R. would be willing to accept major losses if the stake were considered worth while. This estimate must be reconsidered in distinguishing "planned" losses imposed on Russia by aggression and the course of events. In any case, there exists a kind of devastation threshold beneath which recourse to force can be considered profitable and above which it is wiser to withhold the megatons.

1 Albert Wohlstetter, *Foreign Affairs*, January 1959.

The strength of the American reprisal depends essentially on the nuclear charges which would still reach Soviet territory once the United States atomic air and naval forces were attacked at their bases and subsequently in flight, while executing their reprisal missions. At best, even if the Soviet initial assault were signally successful, the Russian general staff would still have to deal with the possibility of this reprisal. Would Washington, if its forces were greatly damaged, retaliate against the opposing demographic system, unleashing similar reprisals, or, on the contrary, would it ask to negotiate? No one can furnish a definite answer to such a question. How can rational behavior be anticipated under such circumstances? And would it even be rational to save what could still be saved, or, on the other hand, would reason dictate inflicting the same damages upon the aggressor in order to bring him to the same level of misery as his victim? And once the machinery of reprisal were set in motion, who knows whether the reaction might not escape all control and reflection? And in that case, how speculate as to what is rational? Washington can answer these questions no better than Moscow, and it is this complete uncertainty which constitutes one of the elements of dissuasion.

Naturally, before indulging in such speculations, an evaluation of the adverse material possibilities is essential: for instance, the scrutiny of the American reprisal forces and of the degree of probability — in the mathematical sense of the word — such forces would have of escaping surprise attack and subsequently penetrating a Soviet defense system that would be in a state of maximum preparation.

What does this American reprisal force, whose destruction is the condition of the Soviet success, consist of? Even today, it is essentially constituted by piloted bomber planes flying at approximately 900 kilometers an hour (600 to 650 Boeing B-52's) or by others flying at lower speeds and able to refuel in flight (approximately 1100 B-47's). Also in service are supersonic Convair B-58 bombers able to be refueled in flight and capable of a speed of some 2000 kilometers an hour during part of their mission. By adding approximately 450 heavy tankers able to refuel these bombers in flight, we have a summary list of the piloted weapons in the Strategic Air Command. To this must be added some dozen of subsonic nuclear warhead Shark missiles, twenty Atlas ballistic missiles which would be launched from unprotected or poorly protected sites, thirty-two to forty-eight Polaris missiles, almost invulnerable when at sea, the planes of the Navy's heavy aircraft-carriers, and lastly the thousands of fighter-bombers assigned to Allied American bases on the perimeter of the Sino-Russian bloc. These last items of materiel do not figure in the official list of American reprisal air forces. They nonetheless exist. Neither their autonomy in flight, nor the training of their crews, nor the explosive charges they carry make them strategic weapons capable of annihilating the adversary at the sources of his demographic, economic, and industrial power. Yet no offensive plan could ignore the thousands of kilotons they would carry over the Soviet front-line targets, nor the saturation of the Soviet defense system which would result from their numerous penetrations.[1]

1 Especially since, in circumstances as dramatic as a nuclear conflict between the two superstates, "missions without return" or missions with bases in neutral countries (as was the case during the attack on Japan by American B-25's taking off from aircraft carriers), cannot be averted. Moreover, this was the only threat to the United States from 1949 to 1957.

Of course, the essential element of the "big stick" consists of the Strategic Air Command, its 1800 combat planes, its crack crews, its forty bases on American territory, to which may be added the installations in Greenland, Newfoundland, Labrador, Great Britain, Morocco, Italy, and also in Turkey, Tripolitania, Saudi Arabia, Japan, Korea, Hawaii, etc. — in all, some fifty other fields where the Strategic Air Command multijets can land or are even stationed.

America has multiplied her defenses against the threat of the Soviet bombers. From Alaska to Greenland, some sixty radar stations constitute a first-alarm belt. Off both coasts of the New World, American naval forces extend the terrestrial electronic watch with the help of surface vessels and long-distance detection planes. Twelve hundred kilometers farther south lies a new detection belt, the "Mid-Canada Line." Still farther south is the bulk of the territory covered by the radar stations. At sea east and west, Liberty Ship radars, Lockheed electromagnetic detection planes, and even special U. S. Navy balloons and Texas Towers[1] permanently guard the approaches to the American continent.

These networks sound the alarm. They condition the functioning of the active means of defense of the North American continent — in other words, seventy squadrons of interceptors, either subsonic front-firing planes or supersonic attack and pursuit planes, and also sixty antiaircraft battalions firing A and H Nike missiles from the ground (the Nike H missiles are provided with a nuclear charge and their radius of action, like their firing rate, is higher than those of the Nike A batteries). This enor-

[1] Radar towers installed offshore, like the oil wells in the Gulf of Mexico.

mous organization is kept in operation by more than
200,000 men of the various American and Canadian services, grouped under a single command, the frontier between the two countries having been suppressed for defense purposes.

Such, today, is the structure and defense of the enormous, permanently vigilant complex of men and machines which must be almost completely crushed before
even relative impunity — and consequently victory — can
be mentioned.

If a small percentage of the Strategic Air Command
escaped the Soviet long-range air force assault, the Soviet
defense organization, which is as powerful if not more so
than that of the North American continent, would act as
an even finer filter, since the remaining American air
forces would be numerically weaker. If, on the other
hand, a Soviet surprise attack were less successful and the
American forces were still capable of a more powerful reprisal, access to Soviet skies would be more difficult to
impede and losses would be inevitable. And very few
thermonuclear bombs are enough to devastate tremendous areas.

Many conditions must be met in order to eliminate the
Strategic Air Command. The first is undoubtedly that of
total surprise. If there were political tension, if the international situation were uneasy, if preparations had been
detected — in other words, if the slightest indication were
furnished — failure would be likely. Consequently a
"thaw" in the cold war, the commencement of negotiations, is one of the conditions the assailant must achieve if
he wants some chance of surprising his victim and consequently wiping out most of his reprisal forces at their
bases.

It is not difficult to create a climate of thaw. A few words, a few phrases are enough. The offensive operation itself would be more complex. The several hundred airfields to be destroyed before the American bombers could leave them are scattered across the enormous extent of the entire Northern Hemisphere. The attack on these airports would have to be made simultaneously, that is, in Texas as in Spain or Great Britain, and the Soviet bombs would have to land at virtually the same moment. If the bombings were spaced out in time, the first explosion would give the alarm, and the Strategic Air Command bombers would evacuate the other airfields. The operation would fail. Not only would the attack have misfired, but its punitive sanction would be dreadful. The U.S.S.R. would have to absorb a thermonuclear attack administered by hundreds, even thousands of planes which had escaped destruction at their bases and could "saturate" its defenses and devastate its territories.

Simultaneous destruction, though imperative, is virtually impossible to achieve — at least by a piloted bomber force. This is because the fields to be attacked are at extremely disparate distances from the first lines of electromagnetic detection protecting them all. The seven or eight fields located in Great Britain are only a thousand kilometers (slightly over an hour's flight) from the zone where the Soviet bombers would be detected — east of Denmark for example. The fields in Oklahoma (Altus Air Force Base) or in New Mexico (Walker Air Force Base), on the other hand, are located virtually four thousand kilometers from the radar units of the Distant Early Warning Line, the line of advanced detection, while those in West Germany can be reached by enemy bombers less than fifteen minutes after detection. These disparities favor the defense system and furnish it several hours of warning. In drawing up its plans, the attacking general staff would have to choose between two equally unsatisfactory formulas: either its bombers would navigate so as to be detected virtually simultaneously, and in that case, those attacking the British fields would strike only an hour after having given the alarm somewhere over the North Sea or the Baltic Sea, while the bombers sent against the Texas airports would reach their objectives four or five hours after the general alarm. The American bombers would have long since been in the air. Or else the Soviet flight plans would be established so that the attacking planes would reach all their targets at the same moment. But in this case, because of the disparity in the distances separating the detection zones of the fields to be bombed, the Soviet planes attacking a field in Kansas would give the alarm long before those sent against the fields in Great Britain were even in the air. In the first instance, the Soviet bombers detected simultaneously at midnight GMT north of Baffin Island, east of Norway, somewhere in Yugoslavia, and 400 kilometers from the Dharan base, might reach the Lincolnshire fields at 01:30 GMT and the Dharan field at 0:30. But they would reach Indiana or Missouri — if they succeeded in penetrating the American defenses — only around five in the morning: in other words, much too late to surprise the Strategic Air Command planes there. In the second hypothesis, if midnight GMT were the hour for the bombs to be dropped, the attacking planes would be detected only around eleven at night east of the British Isles, but before seven at night in north Canada, and the alarm would have immediately been given to the world.

Combined with geography, radar detection furnishes the defense system an indispensable respite. The dispersion of targets in relation to detection contributes to their safety. Of course the figures cited above are only approximate, and penetration tactics can be improved. Combining various methods of reaching Allied air space, the aggressor might restrict the advantages the defense derives from distance. For example, Soviet bombers might escape radar detection by flying low and then save their fuel by cruising at high altitudes once the detection zone was crossed. Or else certain long-distance penetrations could be effected by avoiding the detection installations — even at the cost of long detours — the planes no longer returning to their bases and the crews abandoning them somewhere along the Mexican coast. Another maneuver likely to deceive the American defenses would consist of having all the attacking bombers cross the advance detection zone at the same moment, and then making the planes assigned to destroy the nearest targets "wait" while the others continued on their way toward the remoter fields. Of course the alarm would have been given, but since no missile was launched, the assailant could count on a certain delay in the American reaction, for the threat would remain ambiguous for some time. But since the Strategic Air Command and the Defense Command have anticipated these tactics and a hundred others, a successful surprise attack on the reprisal potential of the American airfields seems virtually impossible. Geography, technology, and the permanent vigilance of some tens of thousands of men scattered throughout the Northern Hemisphere pose an insoluble problem for the Soviet air forces. The dispersion of the Strategic Air Command fields

around Eurasia, like the distribution of these fields between the iron curtain and the Tropic of Cancer, guarantees the "survival" of General Power's Boeing B-47's
and B-52's. The United States air base strategy since 1945
finds its justification here, as do the Kremlin's efforts to
limit their number and proximity.

This reassuring description corresponds to yesterday's
realities and to some extent to today's. If we have reviewed the strategic conditions which still existed yesterday at such length, it was in order to suggest the extent of
the opportunities lost during the last decade. Tomorrow
an impartial history — if the notion still has any meaning
— will judge severely the West's incomprehension and
cowardice.

For in a year or two, the increase in the Soviet intercontinental ballistic missile stockpile will have transformed the situation. Already the first Soviet missiles are
cutting down the warning interval that could once be reasonably counted on in case of air attack. Yesterday, and
perhaps even today, the length of this interval could be
estimated at four or five hours at the least, even if no
other indication than the appearance of echoes on the
radar screens had been received. Tomorrow the general
attack may be more sudden. Even when utilized in small
numbers, ballistic missiles modify defense conditions.

The new studies of the Soviet general staff may, for example, anticipate using bombers to attack relatively nearby
targets in Allied detection zones, and reserving long-range
ballistic missiles for the destruction of the remoter Strategic Air Command bases. Of the American fields that
must be bombed simultaneously, some thirty are located
between 7000 to 8500 kilometers from the Soviet launch-

ing sites. A second series, consisting of some fifteen launching platforms, is located between 4500 and 6500 kilometers from these Russian missile sites. These forty-five airfields are included among those which are farthest from the radar detection belts.

Taking into account irregularities in functioning of the intercontinental ballistic missiles, human errors that might be committed in their use, and missiles being checked or repaired at H hour, we can assume that the number of such missiles theoretically necessary to destroy a specific target with 90 per cent probability must be doubled. In other words, the intercontinental ballistic missile stockpile must be virtually twice as large as the number of missiles to be launched toward the target zone. This figure includes the security margin which the aggressor would in all likelihood allow himself.

If average precision is on the order of 0.05 per cent of the distance (although much better results have been obtained with intercontinental ballistic missiles in the course of their development), we can estimate that the U.S.S.R. must have four missiles in order to be able to destroy each of the most distant Strategic Air Command fields with sufficient probability, and three to reach each of the fifteen fields in the 4500 to 6500 kilometers series. All in all, to achieve a high probability of simultaneously destroying the forty-five remotest Strategic Air Command fields and the bombers stationed there, the U.S.S.R. would need a previously constituted stockpile of some 300 intercontinental ballistic missiles equipped, for example, with two-megaton warheads. Of course, the same attack might be possible under better conditions, but only by taking considerable risks, for no maneuver has confirmed or weak-

ened the validity of these figures and of the operational
extrapolation from necessarily fragmentary tests.

Let us suppose that such a stockpile had been constituted in the U.S.S.R. and that the neutralization of the
Strategic Air Command is to be achieved by a combined
bomber and missile attack. Flight plans would be drawn
up so that the bombers would simultaneously approach
— in so far as is possible — the zones where they would
normally be detected, heading for the nearest targets in
these zones. Of course the general alarm would be given,
but the first missiles would be launched immediately afterward. At the same time, the 200 or 250 missiles in functioning order would be launched, covering in some thirty
minutes a trajectory culminating in the exosphere (the
zone of terrestrial atmosphere beginning more than 600
kilometers above the earth's surface) and landing 6000
to 8000 kilometers from their launching platforms, at the
very moment when — at only 2000, 3000, or 4000 kilometers — the first bombs dropped by the bombers would
be exploding. Hence the duration of the alarm interval
caused by geographical disparity would change from about
five hours to perhaps only two or three. This is still more
than some of General Power's planes need to take off and
escape the enemy explosive charges.

Successful thermonuclear aggression that would surprise
American reprisal forces at their bases is not within the
power of Soviet aviation, even with the help of some
hundreds of missiles. It would be necessary to substitute
ballistic missiles for planes altogether in order to realize
such an ambition.

Since the missiles' speed makes virtually all distances
equal, the advantages America has hitherto derived from

geography would then be canceled out. The distribution in depth of the Strategic Air Command bases loses its defensive value because the speed of the offensive weapon is multiplied almost twenty times, the virtually simultaneous attack on the Strategic Air Command fields becomes possible, and the alarm interval is reduced to some fifteen minutes.

However, the Soviets must build up a sizable offensive missile stockpile to make possible the simultaneous destruction of the American launching platforms. According to the preceding hypothesis, with forty-five fields to be "treated" by relatively imprecise missiles with a low functioning rate, the stockpile to be accumulated beforehand is somewhere between 300 and 350.

While experiments with intercontinental ballistic missiles are proceeding, techniques of direction by inertia are improving and regularity of function increasing, so that if the number and type of American targets which must be destroyed were to remain constant, a stockpile of 350 missiles would no longer be necessary. Furthermore, it might no longer be necessary to destroy *all* the Strategic Air Command bases, provided the Soviet defense system could shoot down most of the American planes that escaped destruction at their bases. But in that case, the Soviets would also have to deal with the tactical air forces whose penetration could considerably reduce defense effectiveness; the risk would be too high to be entertained.

In June 1960, an American periodical published a chart of airfields essential to the operation of the Strategic Air Command planes. According to this document, General Power's domain included some seventy-two fields on American territory, one in Puerto Rico, one in New-

foundland, five in Canada, one in Greenland, four in
Great Britain, three in Spain, three in Morocco, one in
the Azores, one in Bermuda, as well as Enderson Field on
Guam: a total of ninety-three airfields, some maintaining
squadrons of bombers or fueling planes, the others being
used for the maintenance of these planes or for training
flights. General Power was probably referring to this network of bases when he said it would take 300 missiles to
destroy it, his figure taking into account accuracies now
obtained both in the United States and in the U.S.S.R.
But to this estimate we must add the guarantee stockpile
covering the risks inherent in the firing of such a salvo,
the intercontinental ballistic missiles used to destroy the
air forces deployed outside the Strategic Air Command
fields and still capable of launching atomic projectiles, the
missiles launched against the naval forces with atomic
weapons, and, particularly after 1962, those missiles
the aggressor must reserve for the attack on protected
launching sites established on United States territory.
This easily comes to a total of 1000 missiles equipped with
warheads of varying power and having different ranges.

This is a considerable quantity of nuclear weapons,
though well within the reach of nations like the U.S.S.R.
and the United States. It has even been claimed that such
an arsenal will be constituted in the U.S.S.R. during the
course of 1962. That would then be the date from which
all techniques and all strategic conceptions upon which
the American policy of dissuasion have been based would
once again be hopelessly outdated. Steps have been taken
to prepare for this eventuality.

As a matter of fact, the attempt to substitute an effective instrument for one whose power is declining is under

way. The first stage consists of distributing the Strategic Air Command units over a larger number of launching platforms. New bases will also be planned and even built in order to increase the dispersion of planes. The American air reprisal force thereby gains in two respects: the adversary must launch a higher number of missiles against it, and the Strategic Air Command squadrons will react faster, since the number of planes using the same installation and air strip is lower. The alarm system protecting the Strategic Air Command has now achieved such effectiveness that only five minutes after the danger signal, the first bomber is in the air. Dispersion at squadron instead of wing level naturally makes possible a faster take-off for the entire unit.

An attempt is also being made to protect, if not the planes, at least the means of alarm and communication by installing circuits underground and using concrete "armor." Putting bombers under a cement shell would be extremely expensive. Yet such defense measures, relatively effective against the shock effect of a projectile falling near the target, have been studied. By spending about six million dollars per field, the aggressor would have to launch two or three times as many missiles to be reasonably sure of destroying the Strategic Air Command bombers at their bases.

In order to obtain fifteen minutes' warning interval, the American air force has undertaken the construction of enormous long-range detection installations which, upon completion, will consist of three stations located in Alaska, in Greenland (at Thulé), and in Scotland. Each of these stations is to be capable of detecting the body of a ballistic missile up to 5500 kilometers away. Each will include four radar systems; the one lowest on the horizon "catches" the missile and permits its position to be calculated in space; the highest radar system, following the missile's ballistic trajectory, furnishes the calculators the data necessary to determine the point of impact and the moment of explosion. The "Ballistic Missile Early Warning System" will be in operation by 1962. It will give the alarm for missiles, permit the accelerated take-off of the Strategic Air Command bombers, and also furnish the territory's defense centers with the data necessary for future antimissile missiles.

But the Strategic Air Command is not content with this quarter hour's warning interval, particularly with regard to launching its own missiles. It estimates that it will be difficult for a government to organize a thermonuclear reprisal (with the help of missiles that cannot be "recalled") on the information of the radar systems alone and before the enemy missiles have actually fallen on American soil.

Consequently the Strategic Air Command is studying the means of preserving its forces from destruction without depending on the warning system. With regard to its planes, it has planned to maintain up to 10 per cent of its heavy bombers in the air at all times. No doubt when the terrestrial detection system is in operation and the Midas and Samos satellites in regular use, the importance of the permanent warning system will be reduced. Meanwhile, according to the budget plans for 1961, eighty-five million dollars are earmarked for permanent flight.

There is a race for supremacy between the Soviets, who are increasing their long-range performance, precision, and operational security, and the Strategic Air Command's defense measures. But the result of such a competition leaves no doubt that the missiles will triumph. Thus while the bombers—dispersed, protected, alerted — supply the transition, the first American reprisal missiles are beginning to be "operational," in other words usable for military purposes. And new launching installations necessary for their functioning are under construction. The first sites will be in the open air. This will be the case for two thirds of the Francis Warren and Offut platforms in Nebraska. These will receive Convair Atlas missiles. The first Atlas missiles were in the open air, surrounded by their launching scaffolding. Directed by a system combining inertia and radio, they were doubly vulnerable, since they could be destroyed at their base and since their radio guidance system could also be put out of commission.

Guided only by inertia, independent of terrestrial radio installations, the new Atlas missiles are easier to protect. Instead of being installed in groups of nine to utilize the same radio guidance system, they will be housed in individual "silos" and protected by both dispersion and concrete.

In all, some 132 Atlas missiles of various types, grouped in thirteen squadrons, distributed between the Mississippi and the West Coast, will gradually be installed. The Martin, Titan I, and Titan II missiles, of which ninety-six are expected to be in firing condition, will accompany the Atlas missiles.

Static, the 228 missiles will be protected by concrete. Underground installation and concrete and steel armor have been calculated to protect each missile against all eventualities except a direct hit. Even if the fireball of an atomic explosion strikes the silo locations tangentially, the missile will escape destruction.

The dispersion is considerable. At the Francis Warren base, the missiles are to be some thirty to fifty kilometers apart. To visit all the silos now under construction and within the same command one must travel 1100 kilometers. The 450 Minuteman missile force planned by the United States Air Force will be more dispersed and less vulnerable than the first generation of U.S. ballistic missiles. The extent of the work undertaken and the gigantic character of this intercontinental artillery is almost inconceivable.

To destroy an open-air launching platform is more difficult than to neutralize an air base, with its larger dimensions and its planes more vulnerable to attack. The missiles themselves can be more easily protected than the bombers. Testifying before the House budget subcommittee, General Power described the policy he intended to pursue with regard to his new weapons: ". . . we shall protect our sites so that they can first of all resist super-pressures[1] of close to two kilograms per square centimeter . . . In its silo, the missile would not withstand a direct hit from a hydrogen bomb . . . We can do nothing against a direct hit from a bomb or a missile with a thermonuclear warhead." But the aggressor would be heavily penalized if a suitably protected missile site withstood a thermonuclear explosion which occurred only nearby. The enemy would then have to launch a great number of offensive missiles in order to have a reasonable

[1] Destruction by explosive effect; it is the superpressure produced by the shock wave of the explosion which is the cause of the principal damages.

likelihood of destroying even one of the reprisal missiles in its silo.

This number would depend on several variable factors: it is a function of the offensive weapon's precision, of its reliability, of the explosive charge it carries and consequently of the distance at which the explosion would cause an overpressure adequate to destroy or damage the missile site. Lastly, the effectiveness of the offensive missiles also depends on the precision with which the aggressor can localize the installation he wishes to destroy and, of course, on the protection of these installations.

By giving these variable factors the customary values and depending on whether the site to be destroyed is in the open air or underground, though at shallow levels, our calculations provide the following approximate figures:

DISTANCES (in kilometers)	1500	3000	5000	7000
Number of missiles to be launched to neutralize an open-air site	1	1	2	3
Number of missiles to be launched to neutralize an underground installation	1	2	3	5

We are making the following assumptions: that the likelihood of destruction or disablement is 90 per cent; that the precision of the missiles is equivalent to 0.05 per cent of the distance; that the location of the site to be destroyed is known exactly; that the explosive charges used are one megaton and the overpressures necessary to put the installation out of commission are respectively one kilogram per square centimeter in the case of open-air sites, and ten kilograms per square centimeter in the case of underground sites (in the latter case, the explosion presumably occurs on the surface, and the site is damaged by the crater and its immediate effects); finally, that all the offensive missiles take off and that the reliability is equal to 0.9.

These calculations are purely theoretical and can only suggest the number of missiles necessary to achieve specific devastation. Only the Strategic Air Command services which are now constructing the protected sites and are in possession of the results of the atomic experiments in Nevada or the Pacific know the figures which would no doubt be closer to reality. Moreover, the data in the table must still be multiplied by a certain number of parameters in order to take into account the missiles' real reliability and the security stockpile which must be maintained in order to minimize the operational risks of generalized aggression. On the other hand, it goes without saying that if instead of thermonuclear warheads of one megaton, the offensive missiles were provided with a charge of two or five megatons, the preceding figures would have to be reduced.

We have reviewed this material in order to emphasize the influence of protection by underground installation and concrete reinforcement. The fact that the United States Air Force is installing some 700 Atlas, Titan, and Minuteman silos at an average distance of 7000 kilometers from the Soviet launching platforms means, according to the approximate figures of the preceding table, that it would take from 3000 to 5000 intercontinental ballistic missiles, launched virtually simultaneously, to neutralize such a reprisal force. By using more powerful charges, on the order of five megatons for instance, the number of intercontinental ballistic missiles to be launched could be reduced by about half. But these summary calculations nevertheless presume high firing precision, perfect localization of the American silos, and high theoretical rate of reliability. All these estimated calculations are in the aggressor's favor. In reality, it is likely that because of the risks run in launching such an attack, the aggressor would need an even larger — much larger — stockpile than the one estimated.

And even this numerical superiority would probably not be enough to give the assailant all the guarantees necessary. What practice area and what occasion would permit experiment with such missiles, in order to ascertain the effectiveness of such a salvo? How determine the exact location of the sites to be destroyed, the exact effects of explosion on the concrete shells protecting the American missile silos? Yesterday one could prolong the counterbattery and eventually, at the price of an extended and more intense bombardment, destroy the objectives considered most vulnerable. Tomorrow the case will be different. If the first salvo of offensive missiles does not immobilize the reprisal — the entire reprisal — the assailant will pay dearly for his attack. How could he gamble on the effectiveness of a salvo of several thousand missiles, fired virtually simultaneously, knowing that the slightest error in calculation would plunge him into chaos? The penalty would be unavoidable, for there would be no time to limit its effects or to protect oneself against it.

Moreover, to the relative invulnerability of missile sites constructed underground and protected by concrete, the

United States adds the virtual invulnerability of its mobile reprisal systems. The Navy's Polaris missiles, and the Air Force's Minuteman missiles, some of which will be on railroads and some launched at several minutes' notice, pose new problems for the aggressor. This absolute "survival" which mobility assures has its disadvantages, but it adds considerably to the degree of risk the assailant must assume. The Minuteman missiles, which would be launched from their silos before the adverse missiles could land, constitute the best instruments of dissuasion, since they are practically indestructible, though only on condition that the American government determines to base its reprisal — setting off a world cataclysm — on the indications of attack furnished by its Ballistic Missile Early Warning stations. Once again, for the potential aggressor, the danger exists that such a decision has been made.

The logic of the ballistic age favors the attacked power. Even if it still has the means to do so — in other words, if the assault just suffered had not achieved its entire objective — the attacked power could scarcely reply by attempting to destroy the aggressor's launching sites. The latter would be empty — or almost, in which case, the counterbattery would come too late, especially since considerable resources would be necessary, given the high number of sites to be neutralized. And considering the secrecy with which all such installations are surrounded in the U.S.S.R., how can the geographical coordinates of all the missile silos be localized? Consequently, if there were a reprisal, it would be directed against the aggressor's demographic system, against his urban agglomerations and his heavy industry. If the aggressor must first deal with the reprisal forces in order not to have to suffer their effect, the victim of aggression need no longer accept the same imperative: either he comes to terms or seeks revenge. And this is the source of his advantage. Urban targets are much easier to destroy than the offensive missile batteries, which can be dispersed, buried, or mobile. The geographical coordinates of the assailant's big cities are known and the habitat is vulnerable to high explosions, to the enormous "cap power." Yesterday it was enough to launch four five-megaton missiles in order to destroy, with 90 per cent probability, an urban agglomeration six kilometers in diameter located 7000 kilometers away. To-day, with the subsequent improvement in precision, only one missile would theoretically be necessary. A stockpile of one hundred missiles therefore represents a considerable destructive potential, since it would permit the devastation of fifty or sixty such centers. Of course the inhabitants, alerted at the moment of the aggression, would escape the effects of reprisal, but the city they returned to would be nothing but ruins.

It is several years since Camille Rougeron suggested that the nations resort to major explosive powers and gamble on the effects of nuclear explosions set off at high altitudes.

It will be remembered that when the explosion of an atomic charge occurs near the ground, the thermic energy released is about a third of the total energy produced. But the amount of heat increases with altitude, to the detriment of the shock effect, whose strength decreases, lacking support. At the limit, where a relative vacuum exists, there are no longer any shock waves. Taking into account the duration of the emission of calorific energy and also of the absorption due to the terrestrial atmosphere, the amount of heat received at various distances from the explosion can be estimated; calculations indicate that a thermonuclear charge of 20 megatons, exploding 15 kilometers above ground, would release 30 calories per square centimeter at a distance of 45 kilometers — consequently causing third-degree burns. Even if the precision of ballistic missiles were much less than that already claimed, one missile with a 40-megaton charge launched against an urban center 7000 kilometers away would have 90 chances out of 100 of starting disastrous fires.

Supposing that the free world eventually bases the preservation of the status quo on the installation of some 350 underground launching sites scattered over the entire Northern Hemisphere and distributed in depth, a simple calculation indicates that nearly 2000 missiles[1] would have to be fired against the 350 sites in order for the aggressor to be certain of neutralizing them. Naturally, the explosion of these 2000 missiles would have to be virtually simultaneous so that the surprise effect would be as complete as possible. Then too, thanks to long-range radar systems, a certain warning interval — though of short duration — would be furnished which the victim of this aggression could exploit by launching his reprisal. The latter, based on much more limited means, would still have dreadful effects, since it would take only 60 missiles, each carrying an explosive charge of 10 megatons, to ravage 40 major enemy centers. If, in the framework of his politico-strategic studies, the potential aggressor decided that he could not afford the destruction of 40 of his prin-

[1] Of one megaton each and exploding at the surface, so that the launching silos aimed at would be either destroyed or damaged by "crater effects."

cipal cities as the price of neutralization of the adverse atomic forces — and consequently the subjugation of his adversary — he would have to launch not only some 2000 ballistic missiles, but also make sure that such an assault would be sufficiently violent and successful to prevent his victim from reacting with 60 of his own missiles.

According to some American experts, this would mean opposing an enormous enemy offensive power with a "deterrent" cheaply obtained and of apparently dubious value. The preceding comparison of problems of attack with the relative ease of defense is, of course, intentional. Perhaps 2000 missiles would be enough. And perhaps, to achieve world domination, the assailant would agree to suffer damages much more serious than the destruction of 40 of his big cities. But the question of size remains, and that is what counts. Unless there is a new discontinuity in the normal development of technology when, in a few years, the United States will have several hundred protected missile sites, several dozen missile-launching submarines, and missiles traveling on their railway network — in short, when the United States will be using underground installation, concrete "armor," and mobility to protect its reprisal forces — the Soviets could still have an arsenal ten times more powerful without possessing the military instruments of victory. Once a proper evaluation has been made of the enormous margin of superiority henceforth necessary to enable an attack to have any significance, and once it is apparent that the show of impossible force has missed its mark and is no longer believed in, the West must be considered with new eyes.

In discussing the new conditions of strategy, Jules Moch

recalled that America would be "in the first line." Yesterday, there was an "asymmetry" between the Soviet chances and those of the United States, while tomorrow there will be symmetry, the American territory becoming as vulnerable to Soviet attack as the U.S.S.R. will be to the Strategic Air Command bombers and missiles. And in *Le Monde,* on December 6, 1957, the French delegate to the United Nations disarmament subcommittee wrote: ". . . Only just achieved, strategic equality means America's greater vulnerability. As a matter of fact, the American population is much denser than Russia's: 170 million inhabitants living in less than ten million square kilometers, as opposed to 200 million in an area twice as large . . ." And M. Moch added: ". . . Mr. Dulles will no longer declare, as before the days of strategic equality, that in order to defend the peace, the United States must advance to the brink of war . . . Once this equality is achieved, the Turko-Syrian incidents will be settled with the Soviets indulging in only verbal violence, while the Sixth American Fleet, based in the Mediterranean, avoids the hypersensitive shores . . ."

Both premises and conclusions appear inexact. The high density of American population would be disadvantageous to that nation only if, determined to attack first, with preventive intentions, it were then obliged to "absorb" the Soviet reprisal. The latter would perhaps require fewer destructive resources than the American reprisal system would need to wreak analogous havoc in the U.S.S.R. But as long as America pursues a policy of dissuasion, with its corollaries — either a forced peace, or the aggressor's obligation to destroy the American reprisal forces from the start — the greater concentration of population in the United States will not be a handicap. It will produce an inferiority only if, while permitting the Soviets to increase the margin of superiority they are trying to gain, America manages neither to construct long-range ballistic missiles nor to multiply the protected sites where these missiles could not be easily destroyed and from which a crushing thermonuclear reprisal could be launched. We know that this is not the case, and that the arsenal of American missiles is in the process of completion.

As for the consequences of "strategic equality between the two camps," they have not been the ones foreseen by M. Moch. In 1958 the incidents in Iraq, Jordan, and Lebanon provoked more than floods of eloquence, and the United States Sixth Fleet did not avoid the "hypersensitive shores." It landed troops there, for Mr. Dulles was well aware that to protect the peace one must always appear willing to advance to the brink of war.

Favoring the policy of nonaggression, the figures cited above illustrate merely the technical aspects of a thermonuclear exchange. Politically too, it is clear that a reaction to aggression — even atomic aggression — is less difficult to study, to prepare, and even to materialize than the aggression itself. The assailant must confront imperatives much stricter than those his victim will face.

A nation such as the United States, which has renounced preventive — and even "pre-emptive" [1] — action in favor of legitimate defense and with virtually universal consent, can openly take the proper measures to discourage aggression by the threat of a fearful retaliation.

[1] That is, when a still unmaterialized aggression seems probable or imminent.

Without great difficulty, its government will succeed in persuading the population to accept a certain automatic quality of reprisal in order to reinforce the threat it represents. The potential aggressor is not unaware that once these measures are taken, there is a strong likelihood that in case of danger these plans would be carried out. Thermonuclear attack assumes a form characteristic enough so that there would be no hesitation on the victim's part. There would be no time to discuss morality or even the risks involved; horror would be such that the most violent reaction would be possible. At the very least, the assailant would have the prospect of the machinery's functioning without his having time to stop it.

As for the other side — the side studying and seeking to organize attack — in addition to the enormous quantitative superiority necessary, risk attends the preparation as well as the decision.

By doing nothing, abandoning the struggle, no progress is made, though at least there is no danger of being hurled back into history, losing in a few hours results acquired in the course of decades of accelerated modernization. Once attacked, the victim of atomic aggression has the choice of annihilation or servitude. The assailant takes the initiative; whatever the superiority of his resources, however opportune the occasion, however sure his success appears, there will always be a moment when the aggressor, turning his back on security, must risk setting the world-shaking machinery in motion, and without ever being certain he will not be its second victim. Naturally a major thermonuclear conflict seems improbable if not impossible, but it should be more generally admitted that this impossibility results from nuclear parity — of one kind or another — and not from an atomic disarmament which could not be controlled and which, moreover, by confronting conventional forces of unequal power, would invite blackmail by force and subjugation or war as a consequence.

Writing in *Fortune* for September 1959, Professor Oskar Morgenstern observed that it was to the United States' advantage that the U.S.S.R. should also possess an invulnerable reprisal force. The reasoning is faultless: the United States expects a Soviet attack; alarming echoes are detected on the radar screens which derive, as it happens, from meteorites, satellite debris, and various electrical phenomena. Considering the speed at which ballistic missiles travel, there is no time to verify the origin of these echoes. If the order is not given to launch the American missiles, and if these radar echoes did, in fact, originate in a Soviet attack, the reprisal force would be annihilated, since it is not invulnerable. If, on the other hand, the order is given and the reprisal missiles launched, they cannot be recalled to their point of departure. The Soviet territory would be attacked — and partly destroyed — on a false alarm. Henceforth, Morgenstern continues, the same thing is true of both sides. When one side's reprisal force is vulnerable to the other's attack, an accidental thermonuclear war is not impossible. Consequently it is to the United States' own interest that the U.S.S.R., like the United States, should have a dissuasion force of invulnerable power. Knowing that this dissuasion force would "absorb" a first shock without difficulty, the Soviet government, like the American government, would make use of it only in the case of manifest aggression and in particular after the fall of the first enemy missiles. In this way, the danger of a ruinous war neither side wanted would be averted.[1]

But above all, if this reprisal force could not be destroyed at its bases, its very invulnerability would impose the abandonment of all notions of aggression, since by pressing the attack button the aggressor would at the same time activate the reprisal.

Consequently, the logic of nuclear strategy, if it condemns defensive armament and tactics, accords the advantage to the side which, provoked first, would strike second. This form of security is not acquired cheaply. It demands enormous effort, permanent vigilance, and the firm determination to resort to force if necessary. But it can be singularly effective for the nation practicing it.

On the other hand, this same nuclear logic weakens the policy of dissuasion when it is practiced to the advantage of a third party.

If, relying on their superiority in conventional forces and gambling on Western hesitation over the use of low-power atomic explosives, the Soviets were to invade the territories of Western Europe, Washington, as the guaranteeing power, would be faced with the following delemma:

Either the American retaliation would attempt to destroy the major Soviet urban centers, which would not prevent the Soviet strategic forces from ravaging American territory;

Or the Strategic Air Command would first attempt to

1 As a matter of fact, it will be possible to disintegrate the ballistic missiles in flight, so that if there were an "error," they would fall inert and non-active. Such a guarantee, analogous to the bombardiers' *fail safe* system, is not technically impossible to establish.

neutralize the Soviet reprisal force. But in this latter case, the Strategic Air Command would find itself in the aggressor's difficult position of having to conduct a counterbattery requiring enormous resources and all the more surely doomed to failure since the Soviets would have shielded their own potential striking force from the American reaction. Virtually unrealizable when the aggressor has the advantage of surprise, the American counterbattery would have to be directed against an adversary prepared to limit its effects.

Fortunately the nature of the risk involved in attacking the West weakens the rigor of ballistico-nuclear logic. Even by exploiting this new logic to the full, the irrational factor remains a grave danger. The "exorbitant risk" that justifies the national policy of dissuasion still preserves a certain meaning when dissuasion protects third parties. But in that case, the "balance of terror" is precarious.

A simple reasoning based on technological facts suffices to exclude the hypothesis of a generalized thermonuclear war — on condition, of course, that peace is imposed by the threat of such a war. This summary analysis accentuates a certain number of apparently paradoxical propositions.

Taking the initiative in a thermonuclear aggression is, in short, more difficult and requires much more preparation than discouraging such an initiative.

But the side on the defensive must keep its forces in a state of permanent vigilance. It is this side which, fearing a surprise attack, is constantly obliged to protect its reprisal missiles from destruction. In short, the side on the defensive must unceasingly deploy a military activity greater than that of the potentially offensive side.

For its own security, the United States must desire the potential of Soviet dissuasion to be as invulnerable as its own.

Lastly, in security questions, no sooner has one satisfactory formula been developed and the concept of collective defense been translated into facts, than the development of new armament techniques limits its validity. The attempt to constitute a power strong enough to impose respect by the close association of free nations meant merely drifting with the current. Hence, by its possible conditions of use, the new nuclear armament risks weakening a proposition hitherto indisputable and to which the free world is already greatly indebted.

II PEACE, SUBVERSION OR EXCESSIVE RISKS

It will not be long before we may have to give up war altogether. The atomic weapons recently tested and soon to figure in the panoplies of the major powers could enforce the world-wide substitution of discussion for attack.

Up till now the application of a policy of "dissuasion by threat of thermonuclear reprisal" has been confined to the protection of a few vital objectives. Today weapons are being created capable of greatly expanding the zone in which such a concept will become valid.

Since Hiroshima, a generalized conflict has been avoided because every power knows that the cost of resorting to force would have no relation to the slender advantages it would afford. On the other hand, the risk of attacking lesser objectives is feasible, provided such ambitions are modest enough not to require the use of an excessively powerful arsenal. The atomic weapon, by the very extent of the ravages it would cause if used, has authorized a certain *fait accompli* policy. On the cold war level, many actions are tolerated today which would once have triggered general hostilities. The expansionist powers are constantly sounding out Western reactions in order to discover how far they can go without running excessive risks. The West is making the same evaluation, but in terms of resisting adverse pressure rather than exerting it.

The disproportion between the value of the Korean objective and the extent of the nuclear reprisal was responsible for the invasion of South Korea in June 1950. It must be added that Mr. Acheson himself, by omitting to specify that Korea, too, belonged to the defense fringe indispensable to United States security, had limited the value of the Korean objective. From the Secretary of State's statement on January 12, 1950, the Kremlin deduced that it would have a free hand in Korea. The Soviets had every reason to gamble on American nonintervention. Although at the time Washington still possessed an atomic monopoly (and consequently the means to repulse any invasion effected by conventional means), the risk of seeing the United States use such weapons in such a conflict, after such official indications of indifference, was slight. Equivalent in power to more than 15,000 tons of TNT, the first A-bomb had prematurely ended a world war of extermination which had cost the lives of nearly fifty million human beings. But such a bomb was hardly likely to be used in the Korean war, since that would mean using it a second time in Asia, against Asians. The Japanese precedent; the clumsy propaganda Washington itself had launched on the occasion of the Pacific atom experiments, boasting of these weapons' invincibility and thereby associating their use with a third world war; the Soviets' Stockholm appeal, skillfully exploiting popular naïveté; the West's general incomprehension, on the part of leaders and public opinion alike, of the real significance of an American atomic monopoly which was actually providential — all these elements, whether created by the adversary or resulting from the West's incapacity to understand and exploit the advantages it still possessed, imposed self-constraint on the West. Obvious to the Soviets because proclaimed by the opposing camp, this constraint was a primary factor in the North Korean aggression. Later it invited Chinese invervention. Peking gambled that the West would not use a weapon which would have eliminated any advantages China could derive from its numerically superior forces and the proximity of their sources of supply. And subsequent events proved Peking to have been correct. A conflict that was ridiculous in military terms cost the United States nearly 100,000 men, obliged this country to fight 12,000 kilometers from its principal bases and to extend its supply lines across the Pacific Ocean. It is true that Europe had added its pressure to the American self-constraint, for Europe feared — or claimed to fear — an extension of the conflict. Yet at the time, since the American atomic monopoly was complete, Washington could have imposed its will with impunity. America's European allies noisily voiced their quite unjustified outrage and tugged at Uncle Sam's coattails to convince him to pursue the struggle under conditions particularly detrimental to him. Five years after Hiroshima, the West had still not realized the political advantages it might have gained from its atomic armaments. Its statesmen were living in an artificial world that still looked like yesterday's to them, despite the nuclear phenomenon.

On account of the moral restrictions the West imposed upon itself in this way, political utilization of its atomic monopoly remained greatly limited. For over fifteen years there has been a great imbalance between the Western atomic arsenal's destructive power and the minor points of application Soviet diplomacy has afforded it. It must be admitted that by making every use of its propaganda resources, the Kremlin has been able to reveal this disproportion or emphasize it when it was not apparent. As long as there existed no intermediary destructive power between the 1944 TNT bomb (effective within an area having a radius of a hundred yards) and the Hiroshima missile (leveling virtually everything within an area of 2500 yards), two distinct systems could be discussed. In the framework of the first, the strategist knew he would require tens of thousands of tons of explosive, transported by thousands of planes, to demolish a large urban area. By using the resources of the second, an analogous result could be achieved with a single missile carried by a single plane. Even a reader ignorant of the military implications of this comparison will admit the strategic importance of atomic fission and fusion. He will also measure the enormous difference which existed between the "conventional" system and the atomic system, and will realize how the Kremlin could run risks in questions serious enough to weaken or divide the West but not to justify using weapons of massive destruction.

The strategic and political consequences of such a disparity between offense and penalty would still not be generally grasped if new scientific and technological resources had not already been exploited, thus modifying the situation. Physicists have managed to "descend" the scale of atomic power until there is virtually no solution of continuity between the strongest classical explosive charge and the weakest atomic explosive. In recent years, they have not only experimented with explosives of increasingly lighter weight and smaller volume, but they have gradually reduced their power. During the fall of 1958, the Atomic Energy Commission exploded small-caliber atomic charges in the Nevada desert which approximated, in their destructive effects, the classical missiles in use at the end of World War II.

Henceforth only a psychological barrier remains between the two systems — the molecular and the atomic, between TNT and the explosive charge achieved by fission of the atom.

Thus, once again, the nature of the trials by force to which the West is subjected can be modified.

Theoretically, it is difficult to imagine a conflict during which one of the belligerents accepts defeat while possessing the means of victory, for it need only "rise" in the scale of destructive power units in order to reverse the situation to its own advantage. And the adversary, in turn, could not accept such a precarious situation without also having recourse to his own more powerful arms. Yesterday the pace of battle could crescendo until it had exhausted all the possibilities in the scale of conventional weapons. To cross the atomic threshold meant taking a considerable risk, or at least so it was believed, and generally revealed an obvious disproportion between the causes of the conflict and the damages suffered. Risks and lack of adaptation to the *casus belli* combined to localize the war and consequently to make it possible, even profitable. By taking the initiative in such a conflict, one knew that the likelihood of limiting it was all the greater, the more difficult it was to shift from one destructive system to the other.

Tomorrow, matters will proceed otherwise, at least between the United States and the Soviet Union. If the atomic threshold is scarcely perceptible, if those who intend to use force consider that threshold relatively easy to cross and believe that, rather than capitulate, the other side would not hesitate to shift from one system to the other — if, in other words, an initial skirmish could lead to the thermonuclear cataclysm, then both sides must forego this spiral of disaster.

Of course the reality is more complex than this. Each of the two sides in question could base its decision to continue the struggle on the fears which the nuclear prospect would inspire in the other. Each could hope that its adversary would come to terms before resolving on an exchange of atomic hostilities. Each side would parade its determination, for in this kind of bluffing only the show of absolute conviction can weaken the adversary's will. But the issue of such a confrontation would then depend on purely psychological considerations and no longer be linked to the estimate of a technical or military superiority. From the machine gun to the thermonuclear ballistic missile, each side possesses the complete scale of the means necessary to obliterate the other. The destructive power of the opposing panoplies has three characteristics: it is graduated, continuous, and infinite. To make use of it, starting from any stage of destruction, means to risk climbing one by one the steps which lead to the irremediable. This staircase toward absurdity would have only whatever landings can be created by fear. But who can foresee which side will get frightened first? And how can anyone stake everything on such a wager? Can any objective make a nation run such risks?

If it were a question of gaining world domination by force, if, for instance, the Soviets saw no alternative to such a conquest, it is possible that Moscow would take enormous risks. But in that case, the resources of the nuclear arsenal would be utilized quite differently than by facing the alternative discussed above: either surrendering in time or climbing the rungs that lead to massive destruction and annihilation. A general attack, launched with the advantage of complete surprise and intended to destroy the American reprisal forces as a whole, would limit the exchange of blows and, if the United States had not been able to render such an operation impossible or unsuccessful, would quickly result in a dissymmetry eminently profitable to the aggressor. It would preserve both his essential striking power and his human and economic potential, while his victim, stripped of the former, could only yield the latter to the aggressor.

In the framework of the present international situation, the policy of dissuasion by threat of massive thermonuclear reprisal has succeeded in dispelling such a hypothesis. Can we, then, envisage a conflict whose stake would be insignificant enough for the dispute to be artificially limited? Could a show of force which would mobilize combat means of some power still be conceived, developed, and launched, and be halted by the surrender of one of the belligerents, rather than by new risks? If this were to be the case, it is undoubtedly because the conflict's object would be of such secondary interest that negotiation could readily be substituted for an exchange of hostilities. When the advantages of force are questionable, while its cost and corresponding risk rapidly become exorbitant, discussion becomes inevitable. Of course a localized, artificially limited war is still a possibility. Yet it is less likely now that low-yield atomic weapons exist and each side must weigh the risk it takes in commencing hostilities.

Before the explosion of the first atomic bomb, there seemed to be no solution to the problem of how to protect a free Europe. On May 12, 1945, Winston Churchill wrote the new President of the United States to inform him of his own anxieties: "What will be the position in a year or two, when the British and American armies have melted and the French has not yet been formed on any major scale . . . and when Russia may choose to keep two or three hundred divisions on active service? An iron curtain is drawn down upon their front. We do not know what is going on behind . . . A broad band of many hundreds of miles of Russian-occupied territory will isolate us from Poland. Meanwhile the attention of our peoples will be occupied in inflicting severities upon Germany, which is ruined and prostrate, and it would be open to the Russians in a very short time to advance if they chose to the waters of the North Sea and the Atlantic."

But three months after this letter had been written, the B-29 *Enola Gay* dropped the first atom bomb on Hiroshima. Suddenly the balance of power was inverted, and the advantage passed to the United States. The route to the North Sea and the Atlantic was no longer open to the Soviet divisions. And if in May 1945 the United States, Great Britain, and Canada maintained some 4,720,000 men in Europe, a year later their forces could be reduced to 900,000 men without compromising the security of the peoples of Western Europe. The concept of dissuasion from aggression by the threat of aero-atomic reprisal began to take shape and, in any case, the Soviets were quite aware of the dangers which a Western military advance might henceforth assume for them. They were probably more aware of the risks of such an operation than the West itself, for the latter was still divided and uncertain as to the power of its new arsenal.

For almost fifteen years, forcing an adversary to abandon the use of his numerical superiority by threatening him with nuclear reprisal has been possible only in certain circumstances and to the advantage of certain privileged nations.

Simplifying somewhat, one might say that after Hiroshima and seen from the Kremlin, the world seemed to be divided into three major zones. The first comprised a reserved, unassailable domain guaranteed by the United States, which would have risked using its nuclear weapons if a specific threat had been directed against the integrity of the territories or against the sovereignty of the nations included within this zone of total security. The second was a zone of vague outlines whose very nature was ill-defined. The uncertainty permitted both sides to maneuver in it without losing face. The Soviets had to weigh the coveted territories against the inevitable risks, while for the Americans resistance to Communist expansion depended on the circumstances of the moment. The third zone included the nations in whose defense it was obvious that no one would fight, neither with conventional means nor by brandishing the threat of atomic weapons. We

know the role these lines of demarcation have played
and what has become of the zones either not guaranteed
or poorly guaranteed.

The Soviets had used the struggle against the Third
Reich to justify the absorption of a large portion of
Europe. Despite American atomic armament, ninety million Bulgarians, Rumanians, Germans, Poles, Hungar-
ians, and Czechs passed under Communist control. The
Kremlin hastened to take advantage of the Western governments' lack of foresight, their ineptitude in dealing
with the new logic of the atomic era, and also the inertia
of nations eager for comfort after the years of ordeal. The
moral and psychological limitations with which the West
hedged its nuclear monopoly invited one affront after another: the Soviets soon realized that if the new, all-powerful arsenal was ever to be brandished — or even used — it
would only be to defend objectives that were absolutely
vital. It could not be mobilized and would not be even
mentioned in order to insure the protection of apparently
secondary interests. It was essential to act as soon as possible, before the West realized the possibilities of the
magical weapon it alone possessed, in order to seize all objectives of secondary order. The more skillfully Soviet intervention was practiced, the more it combined popular
revolution with internal political struggle, even more or
less free elections, the less reason Washington would find
to use its new weapon.

It was not until the Communists seized Czechoslovakia
that the free world as a whole realized the inadequacy of
its atomic force when faced with the forms Soviet expansionism was assuming. Not that the West lacked material
means to enforce a roll-back policy. Such means were

in readiness. But the desire to use them for these ends did not exist, and Stalin, after the months of anxiety that followed the explosion in New Mexico and those of Hiroshima and Nagasaki, soon realized the opportunity the Western powers' attitude offered him. Of its own accord the free world neutralized the advantages its scientific achievements had won for it.

Since ideology, moral constraint, formalism, pusillanimity, even real terror paralyzed the West, since no affront seemed to merit the Great Penalty, since the policy of dissuasion was not used to forestall encroachment, subversion, and political action, a substitute would have to be found for it. In October 1948, Walter Lippmann wrote in the *New York Herald Tribune:* "While it is preparing its own defensive organization, Europe is protected only by our capacity to dissuade the Kremlin from hurling the Red Army westward, and not by the possibility — which we do not have — of stopping this army.[1] The crucial question is whether the dissuasive power represented by the American air and naval forces will be sufficient, despite the effort which must be made to arm Western Europe at the same time. We must not underestimate this additional effort. At the present time, the balance of power which preserves the peace is a precarious one, based

[1] Walter Lippmann here fails to allow for the use of the American atomic stockpile against conventionally armed forces. It is apparent that the power of the Soviet armored units would be greatly limited if these units, threatened by atomic weapons, had to be dispersed, made lighter and more mobile. In military terms, Lippmann's reasoning is not conclusive. He should have said that since the desire to resort to atomic weapons was not obvious, and since their dissuasive power was not admitted by the Soviets, it was necessary to supplement them with the conventional forces alone capable of making the conflict serious enough to justify recourse to atomic weapons.

on the fact that we can bomb the Soviet cities while the Red Army can invade the cities of Western Europe. But if effective measures were taken to arm Western Europe, the balance of power would be shifted to the Russians' disadvantage. Their cities would still be vulnerable to the atom bomb, but the urban centers of Western Europe would no longer be at the mercy of the Russian infantry."

By its incapacity to utilize its atomic monopoly, by failing to pursue a roll-back policy — which was nevertheless the Soviet policy, despite their evident military inferiority, notably during the 1945-54 period[1] — the West abandoned any attempt to maintain the status quo in Europe. At the time, the United States' missile stockpile was no doubt too small to represent a destructive power at least equivalent to the advantages the Soviet would have gained from the occupation of the entire European isthmus. In addition to the American atomic forces based in Europe and under Washington's exclusive command, conventionally armed European forces would have been necessary in order to defend European territory, to symbolize Europe's desire to protect itself, and to help defray the costs of such a defense. But above all, these conventional forces were necessary in order to make the conflict that had all of Western Europe at stake so serious that the use of American nuclear weapons would somehow be justified, so that it would be plausible, even necessary for America to use her atomic power. Resorting to weapons of massive destruction would be all the more likely since American units would be included among the land divisions thus prepared and deployed

[1] When they scored their most spectacular successes in the East as in the West.

before the iron curtain, playing the role of hostages and reinforcing the guarantee of atomic intervention implicitly given to Europe.

Thus the presence of European and American non-atomic forces in the West's collective defense system would implement the policy of dissuasion, although America pursued that policy to the advantage of other nations than herself and although America alone possessed the means to execute it.

Since Walter Lippmann's article was written, over a decade ago, the defense of Western Europe has not been based on any other concept. After the Lisbon Conference, in which military experts and economists differed, the former asking for much more than the latter could give, it was obvious that the NATO countries could never muster enough conventional forces to "discourage the aggressor." A powerful nuclear armament was necessary in order to confront the Soviets with the celebrated alternative: either peace and a social and economic rivalry, or atomic war and universal destruction.

In order to resist more readily "as far East as possible" and particularly so that the Soviets would have no doubt as to American intervention in its behalf, NATO announced that it would resort to atomic weapons itself, whatever form of warfare the aggressor might employ — whether in case of a general attack or of a threat against one of the member nations, and whether this threat or attack was atomic or "conventional." In December 1954, the corresponding plans of operations were approved by the member nations. Thereafter, NATO's military leaders, well provided with atomic weapons, insisted on maintaining conventional forces sufficiently numerous to "discourage aggression of secondary importance in Europe" and also to increase the value of the European stake by the serious nature which any act of hostility toward it would inevitably assume. The NATO military leaders assume that once they can complement any show of force with enough large land units, it is also plausible to use weapons of massive destruction. Hence the risk of entering that spiral of disaster would be a large one.

Once NATO can convince the Soviets that a European conflict could not be limited in extent, since a thermonuclear exchange is likely from the first confrontation, it becomes essential to maintain the status quo: even with all of Western Europe as the stake, the risk would be exorbitant.

The policy of dissuasion is therefore valid for Western Europe, but on condition that the armed forces deployed there constitute the percussion cap of a thermonuclear system whose use neither side may provoke. These armed forces complement the atomic means, whose dissuasive power they extend in the "low ranges" of a trial by force, where heavy armament could not be wielded precisely because of its enormous power. This is the defensive doctrine, adopted in 1953 and 1954, on which the protection of Western Europe has been based.

Since 1954, the West has grown aware that it has lost the atomic monopoly of which it had made such poor use. Not that the new equilibrium between the United States (with its major nuclear arsenal) and the U.S.S.R. (whose stockpiles were still incomplete) jeopardized the value of the policy of dissuasion. According to the experts, the Soviet nuclear possibilities, limited, moreover, by the lack of suitable "carrying vehicles," merely obliged the American Strategic Air Command, the sole instrument of the policy of dissuasion, to protect its forces wherever they were stationed against a possible Soviet surprise attack. The Pentagon estimated that if the potential air reprisal could not be destroyed on its bases, its power remained unimpaired and the concept of the "deterrent" would still be valid. For Western public opinion, the American head start was decisive; still relying on the virtues of numerical superiority, it credited the United States with forces more numerous and more powerful than those of the U.S.S.R., and consequently betrayed no anxiety.

In practical terms, United States territory was not vulnerable to the Soviet offensive means, and the status quo in Europe depended on an American guarantee all the easier to give since the sources of an American reprisal were beyond Soviet reach.

But the technological *données* have considerably altered, and with them the instruments of international policy.

First the American atomic monopoly, later the joint possession of the nuclear weapon, as well as the modifications of the strategic arrangements on either side — all these situations were accompanied, in laboratories, factories, and on launching platforms, by new scientific discoveries, new technological successes. The atomic explosive's weight and unwieldiness were so reduced that the new charge could be adapted to shells and missiles. Consequently the ballistic missile was the object of unprecedented military interest. More than 4000 V-2's with TNT explosive charges had been launched against London and its suburbs without affecting the course of military events; if only one of them had been furnished with a thermonuclear or even an atomic warhead, everything would have been changed.

At the same time that the American physicists were reducing the explosive's weight and dimensions, they also managed to "descend" in its power scale in order to manufacture atomic warheads approximating the heavy TNT charges used at the end of World War II.

This double development has had important strategic consequences; it has determined a new phase in East-West relations. But the effects of these two technological transformations are contradictory. The former completely alters the situation of the United States, which is now as vulnerable as any European nation, while the latter obliges the renunciation of any kind of armed conflict, no matter how limited, at least between the two Great Powers in possession of the complete atomic panoply.

In August 1957 Mr. Khrushchev announced that the U.S.S.R. possessed ballistic missiles capable of transporting a thermonuclear charge thousands of kilometers. No doubt the American intelligence services knew that the Soviets were building such missiles and above all that they were beginning to experiment with them. Radar screens can follow their trajectory at high altitudes, permitting specialists to determine their chief characteristics. Failing to grasp the significance of Mr. Khrushchev's announcement, public opinion remained indifferent.[1] But early in October of the same year, the first Sputnik was put into orbit. There could be no more spectacular way

[1] Though on September 4, 1957, Stewart Alsop wrote, in the *New York Herald Tribune* that "it is not difficult to foresee that the Soviets will take every opportunity to blackmail the United States and lead it to a Super-Munich."

of proving to the world the truth of the preceding August's declaration. With regard to both propulsive power and accuracy of control, it was obvious that the Soviets now possessed the techniques necessary to manufacture long-range ballistic missiles.

Just as Blériot's flight meant the end of the British Isles' invulnerability, the first ballistic missiles, however inexact, however unpredictable, put an end to the total security the United States had enjoyed since 1812. The overthrow of a situation which had seemed likely to endure indefinitely is never grasped by everyone immediately and in all its implications. The military leaders responsible for United States defense, certain American or British statesmen and a few experts on security matters realized the significance of the U.S.S.R.'s future military possibilities. Undoubtedly, these prospects were not unconnected with Mr. Kennan's BBC speech nor with the opinions of certain specialists who recommended greater prudence in the conduct of world affairs and less recklessness about making guarantees to friendly nations. Of course, aside from the virtually religious sense of her duty to safeguard humanity, America's awareness of her enormous power and virtual invulnerability has helped her face Soviet expansionism. Henceforth, a new factor would have to be considered: the risk not only in sending soldiers to fight in distant theaters, but in offering the adversary (who could henceforth reach it) the tremendous target of America's demography and her industrial and economic wealth. We shall see below the results which awareness of this terrible danger have had on American public opinion. In the realm of fact, and provided the United States takes certain measures well within its grasp,

nothing has altered. Or rather, yesterday American invulnerability was a natural resource resulting from geography, whereas tomorrow it can only be achieved artificially. Henceforth, for instance, Washington must indicate
that it will use long-range ballistic missiles (which cannot be destroyed at their launching sites) against any
aggressor. What is involved is a traditional dissuasion
policy, but with a new condition: vulnerability to attacks
on American national territory.

The self-confidence of American public opinion with
regard to its security and the inviolability of its air space
and territory will be replaced by permanent anxiety. Like
the peoples of Europe, at grips with each other for centuries and seeking a *modus vivendi* despite invasion and
destruction, America must adopt a diplomacy of preservation.

This modification of American psychology will affect
the validity of the policy of dissuasion, particularly when
this policy must be pursued in behalf of a third party.

If the addition of ballistic missiles to the Soviet arsenal
can have such important consequences and can be so
dangerous, the generalization of low-caliber nuclear missiles must, on the other hand, prevent recourse to armed attack, reinforce the strategy of a defensive power and,
assuming unanimity as to its means and ends, justify any
strictly defensive coalition.

The influence of this technological development is already perceptible. By considering the "minor wars" since
1945 during which the two ideologies confronted each
other, we discover that the power of the weapons used
crescendoed until the end of the Korean conflict and then
decreased. During the Markos rebellion in Greece, government forces launched, at most, light bombs against

their enemies, while in Korea, when the American air force used its "Superfortresses" for bombing, the marines transformed outdated pursuit planes into robot planes, loaded them with several tons of TNT, and teleguided them to their targets. If the importance of a conflict was measured by the "unitary power" of destruction normally employed, one could say that, after World War II and the attack on German targets with bombs weighing some ten tons, the Korean war had reached a maximum gravity.

But once the American physicists managed to reduce the atomic missile's radius of destruction, the American arsenals began to stockpile low-power fission missiles. Henceforth there was a danger that these would be used on the battlefield. Advantageous as localized conflicts had been for the Soviets, who could count on the numerical superiority of their satellites, such conflicts could now backfire: heavy battalions were neutralized by low-power atomic explosives and an intervention such as China's in Korea could have been speedily transformed into a defeat. If, four or five years after the invasion of South Korea, Moscow and Peking had contemplated a similar operation, they would have had to take into account an eventual utilization of low-power atomic weapons. And in that case, the aggressors would have the following alternatives: to surrender to the power of the new weapons or run the risk that each side might use increasingly powerful missiles until the struggle escaped all control, concluding in a thermonuclear exchange whose effects would obviously be quite unrelated to the goals initially pursued. Consequently the wiser course would be to abandon a form of war condemned in advance by the development of nuclear weapons.

For aggression to remain effective, it must be prepared

and executed discreetly enough to afford the United
States no occasion to make use of its weapons, even if
these start with only machine guns and grenades. Now
that the difference between high-caliber conventional
weapons and the new low-power atomic missiles is so
slight, no one can tell where a conflict over an apparently
minor issue would stop, nor, more significantly, could
either of the two belligerents gamble with any certainty
on the other's surrender before it had used all the resources in its arsenal. And since, in the United States as
well as in the U.S.S.R. this arsenal includes weapons of
virtually infinite power, their use must be avoided at
any cost.

It will be objected that during the limited conflicts
that characterized the postwar period, not all the destructive possibilities of conventional weapons were exploited.
Hence even if low-caliber atomic missiles had existed,
they might not have been employed. The fact that physicists have erected a bridge between the molecular and
nuclear systems would therefore change nothing, since
either material impossibility or discretion has confined
the belligerents well within the destructive powers they
possessed. Neither in Korea, in Indochina, in Malaya, nor
of course in the Middle East was the entire panoply of the
pre-atomic age employed. Even during the critical periods of the Korean war, the American air force did not
use bombs as powerful as those that had been dropped
on the Ruhr, nor was it grouped in powerful offensive
formations to destroy great stretches of enemy territory.
During all these East-West confrontations, of course, the
struggle was generally of such a character that the Western camp always had the greatest difficulty benefiting

from its own purely technological superiority. There are two reasons why the West has not often found points of application for its power: first, the adversary made every effort to engage it in a marginal area and by local forces fighting fanatically for their independence, whether genuine or feigned; second, the West was not deeply committed, for it failed to regard the conflict as a vital one, whereas the opposing forces always did.

That there is no longer any difference between the largest TNT bomb and the smallest fission explosive has consequences only if two conditions are met: the determination to "rise" in the scale of destructive power cannot be jeopardized by the side intending to use force. And the defensive side must be aware of the limitations of this new form of dissuasion. Such determination is plausible only in certain circumstances and in behalf of certain issues. In practical terms, the Korean type of minor war can be outlawed [1] in Europe and almost everywhere else in the world, but there remains a wide array of hostilities not subject to the jurisdiction of this threat of contagion, and these remain a source of danger.

At the end of 1954, the Indochinese conflict followed the one in Korea, and low-power atomic weapons moved out of the laboratory and onto the proving ground: the American State Department's policy began to take shape. On January 10, 1955, *Time* magazine reported: ". . . despite some opposition, there *seems* to have been a decision to use atomic weapons in the theater of operations of limited wars." Secretary of State Dulles said:

[1] With the saving in conventional material, assault tanks and other vehicles, interception planes, etc., that such a modification in the forms of war would involve.

"The present policy implies the progressive utilization of atomic weapons as well as of conventional weapons for tactical goals . . . This week, the chief of the combined general staffs, Admiral Arthur Radford, has declared that the United States was ready to use the atomic weapon to repulse any new aggression in Korea." Thereafter the general staffs attacked the problems posed by a limited atomic war. In most cases, it was conceded that the new weapons of massive destruction could be assimilated merely by emphasizing the imperatives of conventional warfare. If the speed of the armed forces was increased and their mobility improved, if they were more widely dispersed and furnished with more flexible and less vulnerable logistics, then war and the army could look forward to a new long-term contract. As a matter of fact, the psychological and political aspect of such a form of combat escaped the professionals. It is difficult to see any combatant adapting himself to the fall of bombs with such destructive power. Indeed, Lieutenant General Krasilnikov of the Soviet general staff wrote in 1956 that "atomic warfare requires the augmentation of forces, since it increases the threat of the annihilation of whole divisions which would have to be replaced by large reserve forces." But it remains to be seen if the soldier will accept being so readily "annihilated" in the atomic crucible and if, having escaped a first neutron attack, he will not throw himself into the first shelter and stay there.

Politically, it was just as absurd to gamble on a new war — whether large or small — during which the belligerents would still confine themselves, as in the past, to the erosion of their enemy's means of combat and production, when they possessed decisive weapons in their respective stockpiles. For the theory of a limited atomic war to retain any meaning, for such a war to be contemplated and waged, the aggressor must have good reasons for believing that his adversary will capitulate before the exchange of decisive thermonuclear attacks. He must be certain that the rules of the "minor atomic war" would be respected and that when his adversary saw his own front lines yielding, he would not use his atomic power to re-establish the situation. Or even that he would not take advantage of his opponent's respect for the laws of this kind of war to annihilate him in a few hours by using against him all the megatons he possessed.

If the likelihood of such confrontations has not yet been dispelled, if not since Hiroshima, at least since low-power atomic weapons have existed, it is because a transition has been necessary to permit men's minds to adapt to it, like the transitional development of the armament industries toward the satisfaction of entirely new needs.[1] The concept of "dissuasion from limited conflicts by the possible use of low-power atomic weapons" meant the rejuvenation of the army, the indispensability of each service, the increase of subsidies, the study and manufacture of new weapons. After Hiroshima and the use of the "Big Deterrent" combined with only an aero-nuclear force, the small

[1] In 1955, that is, ten years after Hiroshima, a staff exercise was organized which had for its object the study of a French campaign, 1939-40, conducted chiefly in terms of low- and medium-power atomic missiles (less than 20 kilotons) instead of classical TNT explosives. The exercise "began" on September 2, 1939, and ended on June 25, 1940. Some hundred atomic missiles were "launched" in the course of the 35 weeks that the preparations and combat lasted, at a rate of two or three bombs a week. During the criticism of the exercise, the following question was asked: what would happen to this maneuver if, instead of launching these hundred projectiles in 35 weeks, they had been "exchanged" during the first 35 minutes. The answer of the leader of the exercise was as follows: "Such a question is inadmissible. If that were to be the case, I could neither mobilize nor deploy nor maneuver — in a word I couldn't wage war at all!"

atom bomb revived a more classical concept of warfare. Encouraged by the spirit of conformism on either side of the iron curtain,[2] billions were spent not on the radical transformation of the armed forces (which was nevertheless essential) but on the modification of their structure, their armament, and their eventual conditions of use, in order that — remodeled but not transformed — they might appear more capable of waging prolonged atomic operations. In the realm of military thought as a whole, as in that of Western political thinking, everything had occurred as though the atomic explosive were merely more powerful than the chemical kind, and as though the difference lay only in the extent of their respective areas of destruction. Yet the elements of the atomic puzzle were new and did not fit together like the others.

While military advisers were thus struggling to remain on familiar ground, a few more farsighted Western statesmen were nevertheless trying to take advantage of the atomic explosive's new technological achievements. Early in March 1956, Mr. Donald Quarles, then United States Under-Secretary of State, declared: "No possible aggressor must suppose that we will henceforth use our air force and our weapons as we did in Korea. Every aggressor must know that he will be confronted by all the modern weapons necessary to make his aggression entirely profitless." A few days later, Mr. Wilber Brucker, then Secretary of the Army, announced the establishment of a new land unit furnished with atomic weapons and intended to prevent "minor wars." In September 1957, Mr. Dulles

---

2 Soviet technology, with regard to reducing the caliber of atomic weapons, appears less advanced than that of the United States; on the Soviet side, every argument favors the use — at least the political use — of heavy battalions (which is not the case in the West).

wrote: " . . . In the future, it is likely that dissuasion will not be enforced by a powerful military force. It may be possible to protect nations with the help of atomic weapons mobile enough and located and used so strategically that an invasion effected by conventional forces will seem the riskiest of undertakings." The Secretary of State's remarks confirmed the views of the authors of the British White Paper of February 1957. This restored Europe's confidence that its defense would be facilitated, just when it was wondering if it must increase the forces deployed before the iron curtain or adapt itself to a reduction of the length of military service. But Mr. Dulles' views did not convince all the experts. Admiral Arleigh A. Burke, the United States Navy's chief of naval operations, protested, specifying that limited conflicts, "brushfires" as he called them, could be localized and halted only by "extinguishing" them at once, with the help of non-atomic forces capable of immediate intervention. As a matter of fact, the Admiral was not contradicting the statesman. As far as "brushfires" were concerned, small numbers of mobile conventional forces would be enough to extinguish the first flames. Atomic forces of low, medium, and high powers discouraged any impulse to light a really big blaze.

A study of international events since the end of hostilities in Korea shows that the possibilities of low-caliber atomic armament were accurately assessed on the other side of the iron curtain. The incidents in the Middle East in 1957 and in the Far East in 1958 illustrate this new stage in the form which indirect[1] confrontations between the United States and the U.S.S.R. may still take.

[1] United States intervention was "direct" in the western Mediterranean, quasi-direct in the Far East, but the Soviets operated indirectly in the

Having accused Washington of interfering in the Middle East and of inciting Turkey to declare war on Syria, Mr. Khrushchev then threatened Turkey by a reference to the strength of the Red Army and the proximity of the sources of Soviet power. This was in October 1957, when the world was wondering about the scientific, technical, military, and political consequences of the first Sputnik. Nevertheless, the State Department replied immediately that American determination to defend Turkey was unchanged and that the United States would fulfill all its commitments to the Turks. And since Mr. Khrushchev had remarked that it was dangerous to assume that a conflict, if there were to be one, could be localized, Washington included the phrase in its reply, not without a certain humor: ". . . this truth must be constantly present to the mind of anyone assuming major responsibilities in any country." In other words, since Turkish territory was guaranteed by a treaty, the United States would observe its provisions, even at the price of a generalized nuclear war. The Kremlin could have played up the divergences among NATO members, cosigners of the treaty whose interests might have been quite different; in any case, the integrity of the Turkish territory might have appeared to some as out of proportion to the risk taken in associating themselves with the American reply. But on this occasion there was at least a semblance of unanimity. Each power cooperated with NATO and declared itself in agreement with the United States. It is true that the American determination was expressed clearly enough to allow no ambiguity, so that Moscow in its turn realized that the risk was now on its own

Middle East, and it was Peking which dealt with Washington in the matter of Formosa and the coastal islands.

side. And the Turkish incident of 1957 was settled, one might almost say, by common accord between both sides.

With the Iraqi revolution of July 14, 1958, the Western powers lost an ally in the Middle East. Mr. Dulles and Mr. Loyd of the United Kingdom examined the situation in this part of the world and agreed to accept the *fait accompli* in Iraq: they would intervene only if a counter-revolutionary party appeared which might have some chance of defeating the movement of Najib al Rabaü and Abdul Karim Kassem.

But on July 15, the United States Marines landed in force in Libya while two days later the British parachutists landed in Jordan. The Sixth Mediterranean Fleet received reinforcements from the Atlantic, and American fighter-bombers patrolled the coastal strip at low altitudes.

On its side, Moscow declared that "the Soviet Union was not remaining indifferent to events which seriously threatened a region bordering its frontiers, and that it reserved the right to take the measures which the defense of the peace and the concern for its own security imposed." At the same time, major Red Army maneuvers were announced on the Turkish and Iranian borders. But Strategic Air Command atomic bomber units were sent to Turkey, a special American command was established and entrusted to Admiral J. L. Holloway, and finally two additional aircraft carriers headed for the eastern Mediterranean, while the Anglo-American air and naval forces were everywhere alerted.

Obviously these arrangements meant that America and Great Britain accepted the *fait accompli* in Iraq. It had been carried out too skillfully to furnish the Western powers any pretext for armed intervention. Confronted with a kind of palace revolution and the expression — however violent and incited — of popular feeling, the West was obliged to yield. On the other hand, the American and British military preparations meant that the Iraq incident could not be extended to Libya and Jordan without running serious risks. The turn of events in Iraq had not permitted America to intervene, but the American and British show of force in Libya and Jordan signified that the Soviets were not permitted to intervene there or to cause anyone else to intervene either. Each power abided by this "arrangement" and, on either side, confrontation occurred on other grounds than those of open conflict.

Early in August 1958, the pilots of a Chinese Nationalist reconnaissance squadron discovered that two Communist airfields opposite Formosa had again been occupied by MIG-17 units. Less than two weeks later, the shelling of Quemoy began. Quemoy and Matsu, the former about ten times larger than the latter, sheltered about 90,000 Nationalist soldiers, most of Formosan origin.

Referring to the declarations of 1949 and 1954, Peking demanded the evacuation of the islands and the "liberation of Formosa." In military terms, it would have been possible to occupy Quemoy by means of an amphibious operation launched after an air bombardment and an artillery saturation lasting long enough to weaken Nationalist defenses. An analogous result could have been achieved — with fewer losses on the Communist side — by isolating Quemoy by an air and naval blockade and waiting until the garrison surrendered or asked to be evacuated. The success of either of these plans would have given Peking not only the famous islands themselves and a proof of the untrustworthiness of the American guarantees, but considerable prestige as well, at least in Asia. General Su-Yü, then chief of staff of the People's Army of Liberation, chose a third, more discreet course whose success depended less on the Communist military effort than on Western resolution. He confined himself to shelling the islands. Events were to prove that General Su-Yü had underestimated John Foster Dulles' determination and overestimated the paralyzing influence of the United States' allies, chiefly Great Britain. The artillery bombardment could be justified only if it forced Washington to a reaction of withdrawal. Many Western experts declared that these islands were indefensible, that Chiang Kai-shek should never put a garrison on them, and that Formosa could be defended without such advance outposts. But if appearances were against the Nationalist cause, reality did not facilitate the Communists' task. The Nationalist troops were strongly entrenched, and mine fields and powerful, armored coastal batteries protected the land approach to the islands. Effected under an air cover which would have been attacked by Nationalist fighter planes, even by American planes, an amphibious operation could lead to a failure. On the other hand, the artillery shelling presented no risks, and there could be no better way of sounding out American intentions. The bombardment, with the help of some 300 cannons deployed around the islands, would give the Americans the impression that the position was really untenable and lead to the desired result. If this did not happen, the failure was not a serious one — less serious than if the landing barges were sunk or the American Seventh Fleet intervened and went into action against the Communist vessels blockading the islands.

So on August 23, 50,000 shells were fired against the Nationalist positions on Quemoy. The intensive shelling continued for several days. On August 28, a landing was announced. Three days later, *Pravda* reported: ". . . any American aggression in the Far East will increase the international tension and lead to the widening of the conflict . . . The U.S.S.R. will give China the moral and material aid necessary to the fair fight she is waging for the liberation of Formosa."

While the whole world trembled, Dulles answered the threat by moving his pawns across the Far Eastern chessboard. A first squadron of fighter planes reinforced Formosa while a special intervention unit, provided with offensive means, was established in the United States and headed, five days later, toward Taipeh. The fastest fighters, Lockheed F-104's, were also sent to the Far East. The Seventh Fleet was reinforced by the carriers *Midway* and *Essex* and the cruiser *Los Angeles*. These movements completed, the American Secretary of State made his statement: ". . . the use of force by the Chinese Communists attempting to realize territorial ambitions could create a situation much more serious than if it were merely a question of the Nationalist islands and even the security of Formosa. This would be the beginning of a generalization of violence in the Far East, the free world's vital positions then being threatened, as well as the security of the United States." And Washington announced that the Nationalist convoys supplying Quemoy and Matsu would be escorted by the Seventh Fleet as far as

Quemoy's territorial waters. This was on September 4. Until the eleventh, the bombardment continued vigorously, 600,000 shells falling on the Nationalist positions in one day. But on September 12, President Eisenhower, confirming the position taken by his Secretary of State, categorically rejected the hypothesis of an Asian Munich and declared that there would be no compromises. The next day, artillery fire diminished and during the twenty-five days that followed it was reduced, on an average, to a tenth of the intensity it had previously reached. And on October 7, Peking announced the "cease-fire." Early in the summer, Communist propaganda threatened the United States with a widespread military action conducted with the help of Russian and Chinese forces. Once Washington had shown its determination by sending reinforcements as well as by the firmness of the President's remarks seconding those of his Secretary of State, Peking and Moscow suggested that the conflict over the islands was a purely internal affair, a dispute between Chinese factions, and that there was no excuse for American intervention.

Western public opinion had once again failed to understand the nature of this confrontation and the tactics it required. On September 2, Joseph Alsop wrote in the *New York Herald Tribune*: ". . . the threat that hangs over these little islands in the Formosa Straits poses a terribly serious problem. . . ." The day before, in the same paper, Walter Lippmann spoke of "an untenable position." Both columnists criticized the American government for putting itself in a hopeless position. On September 10, a French newspaper stated: ". . . today the presence of the American Seventh Fleet a few miles from Chinese ports is

regarded by the [Chinese] Communists as a provocation . . . Need we add that eight years ago the arrival of
General MacArthur's troops on the Yalu provoked the
immediate reaction of the Chinese volunteers? It is,
therefore, a 'brink of the abyss' policy Mr. Dulles continues to pursue. Such a policy could be justified, however, only if the existence of a nation and the principles
on which world peace are based were at stake. Is this the
case in Quemoy? One cannot help wondering." And the
title of this editorial was "Dangerous Gamble." In England, the meaning of the Far East incident and Mr. Dulles' attitude were no better understood. "In the interests
of the Atlantic Alliance," the chief adviser of the Trade
Unions declared, "it is essential to specify at once and
without circumlocution that Great Britain will not permit itself to be involved [in a war over Quemoy]." In
the United Nations, Mr. Fatin Rustu Zorlu, Turkish Foreign Affairs Minister, added his voice to the anxious cho-
rus: "The situation in Formosa disturbs the whole
world . . . Our first concern in attempting to reduce international tension and the danger of war is to abolish
the use of force to settle disputes . . ." And a few days
later, Mr. George Kennan also attacked the State Department's policy: ". . . Is it necessary for American forces
to be involved in the defense of these islands? . . . Even
if the question of Quemoy does not lead to complete
disaster . . . not only will the problem [of Formosa] not
be resolved, but it is unlikely that the international community will permit us, after what is happening now, to
temporize as we have done in the past." And the former
American Ambassador to Moscow recommended the
abandonment of an "untenable" position: ". . . Sometimes the abandonment of a difficult position, if it is car-

ried out with firmness and authority, can furnish more prestige to the power determined upon such a move than attempting to maintain that position at the cost of efforts obviously intended to save appearances." But early in October, on his visit to Quemoy, Joseph Alsop wrote: "It is encouraging to see Quemoy . . . simply because the reality seems less grim than statistics . . ." and the American reporter added later: ". . . the problem of Quemoy is not as urgent as we might have thought . . . the damages inflicted [by Communist shelling] are negligible . . . the Communist leaders thought that Quemoy would collapse like the walls of Jericho at the sound of the first artillery barrage . . ." In short, the position was not "untenable."

On October 16, under the headline "Position of Strength," Walter Lippmann analyzed the sources of American power in the Pacific, and on November 10 the *New York Times* printed the headline: "Victory at Quemoy." The comparison of the press clippings relating to this incident are somewhat reminiscent of the famous titles that daily accompanied the stages of Napoleon's return from Elba.

The Quemoy incident has been reviewed in such detail because it characterizes perfectly both the nature of likely future East-West confrontations and also the paralyzing influence of Western public opinion and its press, scarred by history and ill-prepared to understand the diplomatic tactics of the thermonuclear age. One technological and strategic factor dominates the whole Formosa question — which is *the* significant question in the China Sea: at present the Nationalist island is impregnable. The Formosa air defenses are so powerful that Peking cannot rely on the success of an airborne operation.

If General Su-Yü — or his successor — were ever to have
a large air transport capable of carrying tens of thousands of men across the Formosa Straits, he could still not
expose this armada to the Nationalist antiaircraft defenses. Very few of the necessarily heavy and slow transport planes would reach their objectives. An airborne
operation cannot be undertaken tomorrow, any more
than it could yesterday, without the previous neutralization of the enemy defenses and without first obtaining air
mastery. An air invasion, even carried out with the advantages of a surprise attack, is therefore not feasible.

The same is true of a surface invasion. Hundreds, even
thousands of craft of all kinds, from junk to merchant ves-
sel, could have been grouped on the Chinese coast opposite Formosa and headed for the Nationalist island,
carrying some hundred thousand men. But the Seventh
Fleet, alerted by such preparations, would have had no
difficulty sinking the Communist invasion forces. Aggression would have been patent, and would have increased
American freedom of maneuver by putting Communist
China in a bad light. If it were not for the precedent of
Hiroshima, the destruction of a naval force preparing to
invade Formosa could probably be effected by exploding
a single thermonuclear missile at high altitude. Who
would protest? The high explosion would be "clean" —
neither the continent nor the islands nor Formosa would
suffer from it. If there were losses, the aggression would
be manifest. Clearly characterized, the aggressor would be
the only victim. Given the present state of the Chinese
and American arsenals, Washington, if it desires to support Chiang and save Formosa for Nationalist China,
possesses the means of achieving this double objective

without risks. It is because Peking is well aware of the value of the contrary policy that the status quo has been maintained in the China Sea. The key phrase of the "threat" code used in the Great Powers' foreign offices to lead up to and away from crises is the one Mr. Dulles pronounced early in September of 1958: ". . . this would be the beginning of a generalization of violence in the Far East, the free world's vital positions then being threatened, *as well as the security of the United States . . .*" To Mr. Khrushchev, who on the occasion of the Turkish incident the year before had threatened to extend the conflict, Mr. Dulles replied that the United States would not hesitate to go to war over Quemoy. America was taking this incident seriously, its military strength in the Pacific was being reinforced, it was determined to hold Quemoy, and therefore, Peking concluded, negotiation was in order. This was when the cease-fire was declared.

Since the end of the Second World War, three periods are discernible, though they tend to merge into one another.

From 1945 to 1952-53, the United States had a monopoly of atomic weapons.[1] Soviet tactics and the West's own incomprehension of the nuclear phenomenon neutralized this American head start. Of course the United States managed to save what it regarded as essential, but had the new weapons been in Soviet hands alone, they would doubtless have been more effective in another fashion.

In Washington, the policy of dissuasion gradually took

[1] The first Soviet experimental explosion took place in September 1949, but it was not until three or four years later that the Russian nuclear arsenal was constituted and assumed a true military — and consequently political — significance.

shape. But it was understood on either side of the iron curtain that only objectives vital to the West would be protected. A new, generalized conflict was no longer possible, and the status quo was maintained in Europe. Nevertheless, during these years of uncontested atomic supremacy, the West lost the control it had had, or the influence it directly or indirectly wielded over nearly a billion human beings. Numerically, the Communist or pro-Communist world shifted from a slight minority to a distinct majority.

Beginning in 1953 or 1954, localized conflicts of the Korean type were also excluded from the list of possible confrontations. The feasible use of low-power atomic weapons on the battlefield condemned this form of warfare. The belligerents could not run the risk of a conflict that would escape all control and lead to mutual disaster. The hypothesis is still valid, of course, only if the Soviets are convinced of the West's determination to use its entire panoply in "climbing" the scale of destructive power rather than to appease and submit. And even if this determination to go all the way were not obvious, its mere possibility would suffice for the policy of dissuasion with regard to minor wars to acquire the same effectiveness as such a policy with regard to a generalized conflict. To pursue a strategy of territorial expansion or political annexation, other methods must be employed — less brutal, more subtle, and in no case likely to lead to classical warfare. The Iraq incident doubtless illustrates one of these methods.

Since 1957 another technological element has altered the conditions of the equilibrium between the two Great

Powers. The territory of the United States is now vulnerable to ballistic missiles whose fall its experts have not yet learned how to halt or avert. A policy of dissuasion based on such missiles readily re-establishes the balance between the U.S.S.R. and the United States. Since the American government subscribes to neither a policy of expansion by force nor one of aggression or preventive attack, it is not necessary for the Pentagon to constitute and maintain an arsenal as considerable and as powerful as the one with which the Soviets must be provided if they intend to use force successfully. As a matter of fact, the balance assured by the threat of mutual destruction is stable — more stable than it used to be in the days of the armed peace, for at that time a calculated risk could still be taken; in case of failure, reprisal was still endurable, whereas today each side considers reprisal to be entirely out of proportion to even the best of causes.

It is in this way that the specter of force has imposed, if not universal peace, at least the integrity of the Great Powers and, to a certain degree, respect for their respective vital interests. Today, by accumulating stockpiles of atomic weapons of both low and medium power, the United States and the U.S.S.R. possess the means of also preventing any "localized" dispute in which they would be involved directly. If the potential assailant believed that even on the occasion of a conflict of secondary importance to himself, the opposing side would not hesitate, rather than surrender, to use its nuclear arsenal, he would have to abandon force as a means of persuasion.

For a democracy to adopt such an attitude, give proof of such firmness, and agree to run the risks inherent in such a resolve, public opinion must support its government. But it is more likely that this public opinion will yield to its anxieties and refuse to confront the dangers of an atomic war on the occasion of a secondary conflict. The policy of bluffing and the diplomacy of a permanent poker game disturb the Western nations, which desire another form of security, perhaps more precarious but less dependent upon an apparent tension.

Based on weak human means but on important and costly techniques, the policy of generalized dissuasion could be effective if Western public opinion were ever to grasp the meaning of the strategic and political revolutions that have occurred in the last few years.

III THE LAWS OF "DISSUASION"

Tomorrow, the failure of the American military policy would be obvious from the moment this policy could not prevent the use of force. Defeat would consist of the exchange of the first thermonuclear attacks, and such defeat would be symmetrical. From now on it must no longer be a matter of carrying out combat operations, but of renouncing battle altogether. The best general staff is no longer the one which has best prepared its country to carry out operations, but the one which has been able to indoctrinate the futility and the dangers of a trial by force. But each side will be more reluctant to accept the risks of a conflict if the other seems better prepared to wage war and more determined to do so if necessary.

This new conception of the role of armed power has been apparent only since March 1954 — in other words, since the American Atomic Energy Commission exploded a thermonuclear weapon of enormous destructive power (a thermonuclear "charge" equivalent to fifteen or eighteen million tons of TNT). The extent of the damage a single missile could inflict reinforced the notion of "dissuasion from aggression" by the threat of aeronuclear reprisal. Since no defensive system could counter the supremacy of attack, even a purely defensive attitude could no longer be based on any but offensive means.

As long as the destructive power of each missile remained relatively weak, each side tried to wear down the other's combat potential or to sap its determination to continue the struggle. The belligerents had time to adjust themselves to each other. Generally, attack and defense offset each other. Each side mustered new forces as well as it could and alternated offensive and defensive phases until the process of erosion had done its work, and one side could exploit the advantage it had finally won over the other.

Using the lessons he believed could be drawn from the First World War and from the results of its aerial bombardments, General Douhet had supposed that by combining classical TNT explosives with bombardment, it would be possible to undermine the enemy's determination to fight or else, by destroying his weapons where they were being manufactured, to paralyze his armed forces.[1]

Until August 8, 1945, the Second World War invalidated General Douhet's notions. This war, like the rest, was a war of attrition. Hiroshima, on the other hand, confirmed the Italian General's suppositions. As a matter of

---

[1] "After such a powerful attack from the air, one can anticipate the complete destruction of the social system of the nation subjected to an ordeal of this nature. In order to end the sufferings and horrors of such warfare, the people itself, impelled by the instinct of self-preservation, would swiftly impose the end of hostilities — and this even before the land and naval forces had time to be mobilized." General Douhet, *Il Domino dell' Aria.*

fact, the combination of airplane and atomic explosive made possible such powerful long-range attacks that no sooner was it put into practice than "Douhetism" was at the same time verified and outdated.

In a war of attrition, anti-air defense had a meaning. The latter wore down the assailing forces and consumed itself at the same time. A kind of balance was established between the two sides which each attempted to destroy to its own advantage.

After the collapse of the French front, Great Britain, unable to continue the battle in any other way and subsequently joined by the United States, resorted to strategic bombing. Since the aerial offensive grew increasingly violent, the Third Reich entrusted General Josef Kammhuber, today chief of the Luftwaffe general staff, with the responsibility of barricading German skies against the day-and-night attacks by British and American bombers and reconnaissance planes. Each month, the armadas of the American Eighth Air Force bombers or the RAF Bomber Command increased their effectiveness by improving their penetration techniques. Against them, the Germans established a powerful defense organization from Denmark to Switzerland, erecting a defensive wall of radar, fighter planes, DCA batteries and searchlights. On each side, every resource of technology, every stratagem was utilized, every sacrifice accepted. After the war, the study of Allied aerial operations against the Third Reich showed that despite the enormous human and material resources of the German Air Defense, despite a careful training for which the very length of the struggle was partly responsible, and though the attacking planes came as no surprise, for the strategic offensive had been pursued day and night, the defense system managed to destroy an average of only 4 to 6 per cent of the Allied planes in the skies over Germany.

Yet this percentage, insignificant as it appears, actually represented heavy losses. If, for instance, 1000 planes attacked Germany nightly and 5 per cent were shot down, then 50 four-motor planes and consequently some 400 to 500 specialists, pilots, navigators, bombardiers, etc., had to be replaced. If the bombings continued at the same rate for a year and the air defense maintained the same effectiveness, some fifteen thousand Allied planes were destroyed. The length of the war made such losses significant: the British and American war industries had to build and deliver replacement planes, and the training schools for navigators had to prepare some 150,000 crew members to replace those lost in a single year.

When, as the result of an error in Allied planning, or because General Kammhuber's services had succeeded in perfecting a defensive technique, the critical percentage of losses increased, the strategic bombardment general staffs grew concerned. The operational research services — then just established — were immediately ordered to analyze the causes of this flaw in the Allied offensive or of this success on the part of the German Air Defense. New equipment and new tactics were immediately tried out by the crews, for the training schools could not produce prepared personnel at a higher rate, nor could the aircraft industries turn out combat materiel any faster. An increase of one per cent in the daily Allied losses constituted an obvious victory of defense over attack. In the contrary instance, the assailant accumulated sufficient reserves to confront a possible technological success of General Kammhuber's general staff. When equilibrium was reached on both sides, efforts were redoubled to destroy it, the German fighter planes trying to shoot down more bombers than the British and Americans could make, and the British and American strategic aviation attempting to increase the effectiveness of its assaults. It took time to do so. The destruction of part of the city of Cologne was achieved during the course of some twenty thousand plane "sorties," which means that the Rhenish city was flown over by some twenty thousand planes before an adequate destructive potential could be dropped on it. The Allies undoubtedly paid with the loss of almost a thousand planes for the damages they inflicted on Cologne in a period of three years.

It has been calculated that the Allies dropped a total of some 2,100,000 tons of bombs on the territory of the Third Reich. More than 1.4 million plane sorties were necessary to transport this "destructive quantity," and it took four years of efforts to carry it out. Everyone knows the balance sheet of this offensive, which includes the destruction of the German homeland, the scattering and underground concealment of a considerable share of industry, and the moral effect of the continuous attacks between 1941 and 1945. This offensive facilitated the Allied victory but was insufficiently powerful to impose it. On both sides, there had been a slow erosion of the available human and material resources, and the issue of the struggle remained undetermined for a long time.

Genesis

To a large degree, the German Air Defense had been effective. It had mobilized, of course, enormous forces, for nearly two million men served in the defense belt established by General Kammhuber, and it had cost a great deal. But it had also deflected considerable means from the Allied war effort.

Since Hiroshima, everything has changed.

By multiplying by several thousand — even by tens of thousands — the destructive power of a single bomb, the nuclear explosive makes recourse to an active defense illusory. To halt enemy air incursions in a proportion of 5, 10, or even 50 per cent would still be insufficient. The corresponding effort would have no meaning, even if the best of these results could be achieved at a low cost in defensive losses. If, for instance, it took some 100 thermonuclear missiles to destroy the demographic, political, and economic structure of a country, and if this country's defense could shoot down half of the enemy bombers, such losses would not be enough to deter an aggressor from launching an atomic war. And how achieve even a 50 per cent defensive effectiveness, when after years of preparation and training the success of the German defense was ten times less?

In recent years, experts studying the defense of European territory against Soviet air incursions have produced disappointing results. It has been estimated that with about forty atomic missiles the Soviets could dislocate and paralyze the Allied system of aerial defense and reprisal. Even with a defense effectiveness of about 20 per cent, it would be enough for the aggressor to use forty-eight planes instead of forty to achieve these objectives without fail. He would deprive his victim of the means of combat and consequently triumph merely by making this minor additional effort. The eight bombers he would add to his offensive air force and would be willing to lose in order to assure victory would not represent in value the hundredth part of the cost of the powerful defensive system necessary for their destruction. It will be objected that new techniques have been perfected which can notably augment defense effectiveness. The use of ground-to-air missiles is becoming widespread and modern, electronically-equipped interceptors would be much more effective than those used during the last hostilities, but — particularly in Europe, where there is no depth — the margin between the most optimistic results the best defensive filter could produce and the small number of bombers sufficient to overpower a large country is such that the whole concept of defense is shown to be outdated.

This was already the case several years ago, when explosive charges had to be carried by airplanes. Within the last two years, the appearance of the ballistic missile has relegated active aerial defense to the status of the crossbow, at least until new techniques are found. Each side is working hard to perfect anti-missiles, yet no concrete results have as yet been achieved. Undoubtedly these defensive weapons will appear in the arsenals of the major powers only after large stockpiles of ballistic missiles are constituted. And even when anti-missile missiles are in current use, account must still be taken of the human or technological failure and the fall of some enemy missiles capable of devastating an immense slice of territory. Although studies of defense techniques are in progress, an aerial defense organization now promises only secondary results: it can make the enemy's aggressive intentions slightly more difficult to materialize and can force him to additional efforts and expenditures, which must be set down on the debit side of his offensive ledger. But we must not expect of such an organization more than it can provide. Consequently we must devote to it only the material and intellectual means it deserves.

Once the destructive level of a single missile or a single explosive charge exceeds a certain limit — defined by the conditions of modern life, by the social structure, geographical organization, and economic and industrial necessities — the "filter" principle, on which defense is based, is no longer of any value. To filter the "destructive quantity" once a single one of its units is enough to wreak excessive havoc is not sufficient. Something else must be devised.

In military terms, the policy of dissuasion originates in this abandonment of aerial defense. After Hiroshima, the United States carried out a kind of world police action based on the fear their aerial atomic force inspired. Order was maintained at low cost the world over. For the American people, this solution of the problem of its new responsibilities as a major power had many advantages. Particularly since the general staffs could prove that once the destructive power of a single missile had increased astronomically, defense was ineffective and had to be replaced by the threat of reprisal.

It is one of the paradoxes of this ballistico-nuclear age that the most peace-loving of nations or coalitions can no longer base their security on defensive weapons. Yesterday it was possible to adopt a strictly defensive strategy and to maintain it with the help of defensive armament. This was the case in certain European nations such as Switzerland and Sweden, which combined policy, tactics, and defensive armaments to enforce recognition of their neutrality. After the First World War, this was also France's attitude, to a certain degree. Only to a certain degree, since France was not neutral but adopted a defensive strategy at the same time that she gave her guarantee to the Lesser Entente.[1] In France's conception of her armed forces, the idea of defense was clearly dominant. The Maginot Line, the use she expected to make of her armored forces, the importance attributed to defense aviation — all illustrated this purely defensive notion which France supposed would guarantee her security. And if, to give herself the illusion of possessing a complete panoply, France developed a small bomber force, this subdivision was immediately called "Defense Heavy Aviation." The designation appeased everyone's conscience.

At the time, this notion of the security that could be achieved by defense alone still had some justification. And with the help of demagoguery, there was no lack of popular support.

Today it is no longer excusable to associate the ideas of the past so unrealistically with the techniques of the present. Quite recently an eminent German statesman admitted that he could not conceive how a defensive policy could be based on offensive weapons. The logic of the period was unintelligible to him, or rather, he could not subscribe to the apparent illogicality of the facts. A truly peace-loving people could not use offensive forces. Since the thermonuclear weapon existed, it could be used defensively and one might even go so far as to "barricade" the skies of the territory to be defended by nuclear ex-

---

[1] In May 1940, we find the same contradiction: an army conceived for defensive tasks was sent offensively into Holland. French rearmament before World War II was marked by a contradiction of another order: allied with maritime powers, France spent a large share of her military subsidies on her navy, as she should have done if, allied with continental powers, she had had to contend with maritime powers.

plosions, but no one must impose peace by wielding the
threat of a terrible penalty which the recourse to offensive
means would inflict. Morally quite respectable, this attempt to transpose to the thermonuclear age a pre-atomic
concept of security cannot be justified by the facts.

Even in the United States, the policy of maintaining
peace by the threat of massive reprisal was not immediately victorious. As long as there was an American monopoly of atomic weapons, United States military superiority
was obvious. This country could have defeated the strongest and the largest "conventionally" equipped armies. It
might have pursued a roll-back policy and imposed
its laws on the rest of the world. If there has been an
equilibrium, it is because political and moral self-restraint
prevented America from taking advantage of her decisive
military superiority. After Hiroshima, and once the first
consequences of the atomic fact were measured by the
governments of the world, a kind of watershed divided
the globe in two. On one side were the nations for whose
benefit it was obvious America would run the risk of guaranteeing their integrity and independence. On the other
were those peoples who did not "deserve" such a commitment.

Yet the United States could have pursued the most ar-
rogant of policies. Without running any danger, certain
of impunity and with considerable chances of success,
America might have changed the configuration of this
watershed and guaranteed the independence of every nation threatened by the U.S.S.R. This advantage was not
exploited. Quite utilizable in the services of an offensive
diplomacy, the nuclear threat was never contemplated
save for defensive ends.

Later, after 1952 or '53, the West readily accepted the loss of the United States' atomic monopoly. It gambled on the head start this country had acquired and on the technical superiority of the new weapons it would certainly devise.

As a matter of fact, six months after General Eisenhower's inauguration, American experts learned of the first Soviet thermonuclear explosion. At the time, the Soviet strategic air forces were equipped only with relatively slow and short range bombers. The Pentagon decided it still had time to establish a powerful air defense organization. This would at least hamper the adversary and increase the threat of reprisal, adding some effectiveness to the general dissuasion policy. Ballistic missiles were not yet in sight, and if a threat was foreseeable it was only the threat of the new Soviet heavy bombers. Given the state of the aeronautical technology of the period, these bombers — requiring enormous fuel loads — could fly only at subsonic speed (at a speed lower than, but close to, that of sound) and would therefore approach the defenses of the American continent at a maximum speed of some 900 kilometers an hour. Against such planes, the interceptor could maintain a certain margin of superiority. Fighting at short range and requiring only a limited fuel supply, fighter planes could fly twice as fast as the offensive bombers hauling their tons of fuel for thousands of kilometers. The American air space would not be rendered impenetrable, but the aggressor's task would be singularly complicated. In order to obtain the subsidies necessary for the development of a defensive system without haggling over the share to be devoted to the Strategic Air Command, which remained the trump card of Amer-

ican security, it was necessary to reduce the subsidies
destined for the Navy and the Army, and to reduce the
manpower of the American armed forces by nearly
600,000 men.

This because, despite her wealth, America begrudged
the cost of her security and that of her allies. As early as
September 1952, during his electoral campaign, General
Eisenhower had declared: "Our big expenditure is the
60 billion dollars set aside for our security [referring to
the 1952 budget during the Korean war]. It is in this
area that the greatest savings can be made. These savings
must be achieved without reducing our defensive power
. . ." and, already a good politician, the general added:
"The bankruptcy of America, rather than her defeat on
the field of battle, is the Soviet goal." This notion had
won over Mr. George M. Humphrey, Secretary of the
Treasury, Admiral Radford, President of the Joint Chiefs
of Staff Committee, and Mr. Charles E. Wilson, Secretary
of Defense. This impact of economic considerations on
military affairs and consequently on the general security
policy gave the doctrine of massive retaliation an additional interest. Costly as it was, this policy was less so
than the maintenance of large armed forces. It burdened
the nation's economy less and suited the American citizen's almost traditional concept of the role of the military:
to animate a powerful technology rather than to be sub-
sidized by it. Yet the enormous mass of Soviet land forces
still had to be counterbalanced. In January 1954, Mr.
Dulles declared: "Local defense[1] will always be important,

---

[1] By "local defense," the Secretary of State meant battle in localized conflicts, with "conventional" means, even low-power "tactical" atomic weapons.

but there is no local defense that can contain the powerful land forces of the communist world. A reprisal force is necessary to reinforce local defense."

Hence both economy and strategy justified the doctrine of reprisal. The decision to abide by it exclusively was made at the end of 1953 with the adoption of a strategic "New Look." The defense budget would be raised to some thirty-five billion dollars and, at this price, would provide a "big stick" capable of policing the world.

Whatever such a policy's actual field of application has been, it seems to have re-established a certain equilibrium between one bloc's aggressive expansionism and the other's static protectionism.

To dissuade the adversary from resorting to force is not a new attitude in the history of relations between nations. The initiator of a conflict, by estimating the risks he ran, could always compare them to the stake of the dispute. Even if the trial by force ended in his favor, it was nevertheless essential that the cost of the struggle not exceed the advantages of victory.

Yet tomorrow a false estimate could be fatal. Yesterday, when a war was over, the vanquished side yielded a portion of its territory, changed its government, modified its policies, put itself in the hands of a new dynasty. Today the risk assumes another dimension. It is a question of the very existence of the peoples engaged in such an enterprise. If there were a conflict, it is likely that devastation would be shared by either side and that the two belligerents would suffer from the use of force in almost equal terms. It is much more difficult to foresee hostilities which would be only unilateral and whose effects would be felt unequally. The smallest error in the evaluation of the adversary's forces and behavior would lead to destruction which, mutually suffered, would be out of all proportion with the cause as with the stake of the conflict.

Naturally it is essential, in this policy of maintaining the status quo by threat, that either side be quite aware of the risks of using force. Unlike the past, and because henceforth it is a question of preventing war rather than waging and winning it, it is necessary that each camp be perfectly informed of the other's potentialities. The more terrible the opponent's reprisal force appears, the firmer the peace is likelier to be. It is even preferable that the aggressive group overestimate the opposing possibilities. On each side of the iron curtain, frequent declarations have reminded the adversary of the power of the thermonuclear weapon whose use he risked provoking. Moscow has vaunted first the numerous Soviet divisions, then the A-bomb, and now the offensive weapons with thermonuclear warheads to which Mr. Khrushchev so often refers. In the West, the power of the Strategic Air Command has been described many times, and its automatic reaction to generalized aggression emphasized. Hence we revert to the old tournament lists, where the combatants hurled insults at each other and boasted of their weapons and their strength before proceeding to a confrontation. But in this case the experts on either side are virtually up to date on the respective possibilities of each thermonuclear force. It remains, however, to influence public opinion in either camp and to gamble on its ignorance of the new laws of nuclear strategy, so that it might weaken, by its horrified reactions, the value of the opposing camp's policy of dissuasion. It must be admitted that the Kremlin, which pays little attention to public opinion, has singular advantages over the free world, whose policies depend on public opinion.

Hence we gradually discern the characteristics of the new policy of dissuasion. To use a mathematical analogy, dissuasion is like a product of two factors, one of which, purely technological, represents the operational value of the military means used to effect retaliation, and the other, a subjective element, expresses the threatened nation's desire to resort to force rather than appeasement.

It is convenient to present these two conditions of the policy of dissuasion in the form of a product. As if it depended on this simple mathematical formula, the validity of such a policy is linked to the value of each of the terms of the product. If one of these is zero, the whole is without effect. If the government of the nation against which dissuasion is being practiced were able either to neutralize the opposing reprisal forces, to annihilate the desire to use them, or to reduce the power of the means of reprisal and at the same time weaken the desire to use them, the policy of dissuasion would collapse. The potential aggressor could then take the risk, after some investigation to measure its adversary's determination, of threatening — and even using — force.

To a large degree, the status quo throughout the world, and particularly in Western Europe, depends on the policy of dissuasion. As atomic armament grows more widespread and other nations besides America and Great Britain gain possession of it, either in their own right or under a "double check," the notion of dissuasion will also become more common, each nation practicing it according to its means. What does it really consist of? What are the conditions of its effectiveness? The mathematical analogy facilitates this analysis. We need only study separately each of the terms of the product to which it can be schematically reduced — that is:

1. The quality of the military instruments of dissuasion, whether the explosive itself or the planes or missiles carrying the explosive;

2. The conditions that must be met for the potential aggressor to regard recourse to such an arsenal as likely.

Elementary Virtues of a Thermonuclear Force

The military means of the policy of dissuasion must be invulnerable or virtually so. They must escape destruction. Whatever the power of the adverse forces, and despite all the advantages the initiative gives the aggressor, the "survival" of the retaliation forces must be assured. It is understood that the nation which bases its security on the policy of dissuasion is not itself the initiator on the conflict. It merely threatens with severe reprisal whatever nation attacks its sovereignty or the integrity of its territories and wealth. It does not use force first. If there is a conflict, it is its adversary which resorts to force. The military jargon of the thermonuclear era specifies that the defensive power must be constantly prepared to "absorb" an atomic shock while at the same time being able and willing to retaliate. To meet the first of these two conditions, the weapons of reprisal must "survive" the assault the aggressor would make upon them.

In isolation, this faculty of "survival" constitutes a powerful dissuasion factor. Why use force or even the threat of force if you risk provoking a reaction that cannot be warded off and whose effects cannot be suffered with impunity?

As long as bombers carrying the atomic charges constituted such reprisal forces, the aggressor might have anticipated destroying a certain number of them at their bases so that afterwards, thanks to a defensive organization operating at the highest degree of effectiveness, he could halt the rest before the targets aimed at were hit. Because the best defensive organization cannot be impermeable to atomic attack, the general staffs count more on ground destruction than on flight interception in estimating the respective possibilities of offense and defense.

The reprisal air forces of the defensive nation must not be vulnerable at their bases, even if the aggressor, benefiting from an effect of total surprise, launched a powerful thermonuclear attack against them. If the defensive side made the preparations necessary to assure the safety of its reprisal potential and the adversary were perfectly aware of the effectiveness of these measures, then the latter could not use force.

Ever since ballistic missiles have been added to bombers, the aggressor has had to gamble still more heavily on attacking his victims launching sites than on intercepting his missiles in flight. To destroy a ballistic missile in its trajectory appears difficult in quite a different way from intercepting a bomber, even a supersonic one. The aggressor must therefore attempt the preventive neutralization of the opposing reprisal force by destroying virtually all its launching sites, all its missile platforms, whatever their number and wherever they are located.[1] Since the dimensions of these targets are smaller than those of

[1] At least as long as the technology of the anti-missile missile remains in its infancy.

airfields, since the missile-launching sites are less vulnerable to the effects of atomic explosion than the air bases, and since, too, they can be buried deep underground or protected by mobility on the surface of the earth or the sea, in space, or deep in the ocean, their destruction can be made virtually impossible. If the protection of the instruments of reprisal were thus assured, and if the potential aggressor, analyzing the result of the preparations made by its eventual victim, discovered that it could not destroy the latter's means of retaliation before suffering their effects, then the status quo would be imposed. In short, for dissuasion to be effective, it is enough, on the military level, that the nation practicing this policy be able at all times to safeguard its ballistic missiles from aggression. Its attitude is strictly defensive, since the object of its military policy is merely to use all the resources of passive defense — mobility, burial underground, dispersion, distance — so that its own forces do not constitute vulnerable targets. Once this invulnerability is achieved, aggression is made impossible because the corresponding risk is too irrational.

In the age of ballistic missiles, the technological conditions of dissuasion can therefore be met more certainly, even more easily than in the age of bombers. Of course nothing could keep the aggressor from annihilating the urban centers of the nation it planned to attack. In a few minutes, this nation could be erased from the map as an organized national collectivity. But if such devastation were not preceded — or at least were not accompanied — by the destruction of the missile-launching sites of the nation attacked, the aggressor would have no time to take advantage of his easy victory. He, too, would be eliminated from the group of modern nations for a long time to come. Contrary to popular belief, the further we advance into the ballistico-nuclear age, the more possible it becomes to outlaw violence, even if the aggressor nation is stronger and more richly supplied with combat means than the nation it threatens.

For the policy of dissuasion to be effective, the reprisal forces on which it is based must escape the aggressor's initial attack, and the aggressor must know this. But these reprisal forces must also penetrate the enemy's defenses and the assailant must be aware that his defenses are vulnerable to the assaults he has provoked.

Possessing the initiative, gambling on his future victim's reaction, the aggressor would obviously mobilize his defensive means before striking his first blow. He would thereby try to minimize the power of this reaction and, if possible, forearm himself against it altogether. The reprisal forces would therefore have to deal with the most efficient possible defensive system and the strongest blockade that could be built. We must consider one factor, which adds, moreover, to the virtues of reprisal: the development and perfection of the aggressor's defensive system could not be achieved without being obvious to all and without thereby compromising the secrecy the aggressor requires in order to destroy the largest possible portion of his victim's reprisal forces at their bases.

The element of surprise affords the aggressor powerful advantages which can be decisive for the success of his attack, but which also impose certain constraints. The effectiveness of the defensive system with which he will try to protect his air space and his territory would result

from a compromise between the degree of preparation he
could achieve and his care not to draw the attention of
his future victim. Alerted, more vigilant, this "victim"
would take measures to protect his own reprisal forces
from destruction. Merely by these arrangements to safeguard his thermonuclear potential, he would impose the
abandonment of aggressive intentions.

If the aggressor nation could set up a defensive system
impermeable to the incursions of reprisal forces —
whether these consisted of bombers, missiles, or even a
combination of the two — all the laws of thermonuclear
strategy would be subverted. The initiator of a conflict
would no longer have to be certain of destroying virtually
all of his victim's reprisal forces at their airfields or launching platforms. The aggressor nation would merely issue
an ultimatum and then wait for the reactions of the
nation thus provoked and threatened. If, rather than
yield to so brutal a demand, this nation were to launch
its retaliation forces against the aggressor, the latter could
destroy them in flight, before they could reach their
targets. On one side, the offensive potential would be intact while on the other it would have disappeared. The
dissymmetry of the remaining forces would obviously permit the country that had issued the ultimatum to impose
its rule.

It could provoke reprisal even more certainly by attacking, for instance, one or several enemy urban centers.
If it then had the capacity to annihilate all of the offensive
forces launched in retaliation against its own territory, it
would deprive its adversary of the material possibility of
continuing the combat, obliging the latter to yield to
the aggressor's will.

In the framework of this hypothesis, the air forces destined to carry out the reprisal mission would not be attacked at their bases, and the aggressor would have economized on the enormous offensive means necessary to the success of such tactics. Vulnerable to defensive intervention, the reprisal air forces would be knocked out before dropping their explosive charges. Based on inadequate means, either because of the intrinsic weakness of their "penetration" power or because of the effectiveness of the aggressor's defensive system, the policy of dissuasion would fail.

Paradoxical as it may seem, a virtually 100-per-cent-effective defensive system — if such effectiveness could ever be achieved — would afford the potential aggressor advantages vastly superior to those he would derive from an extremely powerful offensive force. If he could base his entire aggressive strategy on the impenetrability of his defense, he would need only an extremely limited thermonuclear force (limited in numerical terms, that is) in order to possess the best instrument for a policy of intimidation. Hence the new paradox of this age: the most ambitious aggressive intentions must have a solid defensive organization as their principal instrument.

But such a defensive system is difficult to create, for very few projectiles need to penetrate it to inflict extensive damages. If the aggressor counted on the blockade power of his anti-air defenses, he would have to accept the risk of provoking a violent thermonuclear reaction whose strength he could not filter sufficiently to keep only an absorbable "quantity of destruction" from getting through. Already unlikely when squadrons of bombers carried the nuclear missiles, such a hypothesis becomes groundless

once ballistic missiles are added to the panoply of dissuasion. Indeed, the penetration power of a thermonuclear air force is not easy to limit, and the general staff
that plans for launching the aggression would be wiser to
attempt to destroy the enemy reprisal force at its source
rather than in the air.

If, on the other hand, this reprisal force still consisted
only of bombers and if the number of these bombers
were low, the preceding statement would have to be
modified. The potential aggressor would adopt another
strategy, gambling on the initial destruction of a part of
the enemy bombers, which he would attempt to surprise
at their airfields, and on the blockade power of his own
defense system. Even if this defense system were far
from impermeable, it would afford quite satisfactory
results, since its means could be concentrated on the several air incursions of reprisal forces that escaped the aggressor's first attacks on their airfields.

When the chief of the Strategic Air Command asks for
an increase in the number of his bomber squadrons, it is
not because they cannot carry an adequate "quantity of
destruction." What General LeMay wanted and what his
successor, General Power, now demands, is a reprisal air
force which, once the materiel lost during the attack on its
bases by the Russian strategic forces has been discounted,
can still "saturate" the Soviet air space defenses, and which
still represents a destructive potential proportionate to the
enormous stake the United States constitutes.

The various elements which enter into such a calculation are necessarily uncertain, subject to change, and
difficult to measure. Since so many things depend, nevertheless, on their evaluation, important security margins

must be allowed on either side. The destructive potential the Strategic Air Command bombers could carry is thus considerable, even "superabundant." Even in the hypotheses most unfavorable to their capacities to "survive" the initial assault and penetrate the Soviet air defenses, the American bombers would still be capable of transforming the Russian territory into a desert.

This might be the case even today. The first Soviet operational missiles do not modify the strategic equation on which the entire policy of dissuasion has been based for the last fifteen years. These missiles are neither numerous, reliable, nor precise enough to destroy the entire American reprisal air force at its bases. A general offensive against this force would have to combine bomber potentialities with those of the Soviet missiles. And warning indications would then be furnished which would permit the Strategic Air Command to safeguard at least a part of its squadrons.

But it there were a real dissymmetry in the means of aggression and reprisal, the latter being constituted by squadrons of bombers and the former by an arsenal of ballistic missiles, equilibrium might be singularly precarious. Vulnerable at their bases and also in flight, the reprisal bombers would not necessarily inspire sufficient fear to play their role and impose peace.

Employing his ballistic missiles, the aggressor would have no difficulty destroying the reprisal forces, or at least the essential part of these forces, at their airfields. Surprise would be a further advantage to the aggressor, who would simultaneously launch a large number of ballistic missiles. The victim's reprisal planes escaping this attack would be faced by the aggressor's defense system, and since the number of these planes would necessarily be limited by the success of the initial assault, the aggressor's defense system would have a certain effectiveness and it is likely that the victim's reprisal forces would be annihilated before having inflicted much damage. This is the notion advanced by Albert Wohlstetter, in *Foreign Affairs*, January 1959,[1] in a discussion of a possible U.S.S.R.-U.S.A. conflict.

Supposing that the reprisal forces were numerically much smaller, as is the case, for instance, in Great Britain, we can question the value of a policy of dissuasion with instruments so uncertain. For the Bomber Command to escape the few Soviet ballistic missiles sufficient to annihilate it, a permanent alert, costly measures of dispersion in space, even semipermanent flight, are requisite. The bombers that would not be knocked out at their bases by the blast of a thermonuclear explosion would then have to penetrate an alerted Soviet defense system concentrating its means on a small number of air incursions, since, in any case, the Bomber Command forces are numerically quite modest. They are qualitatively modest as well, for they comprise subsonic material designed a decade ago. A policy of dissuasion based on such precarious military potentialities was of value only as long as the threat itself was also materialized by a bomber force. If the British air bases were vulnerable to the attacks of these bombers, at least, the United Kingdom Air Defense could count on an alert long enough to permit a part of the Bomber Command to escape de-

---

[1] Wohlstetter emphasizes the dangers of complacency with regard to the American technological head start and shows that a balance of terror between the two superstates remains precarious.

struction. But above all, during this period the American territory was practically out of reach, its invulnerability constituting the best guarantee of British security. Such solidarity made the free world into an impregnable bloc. Protected by the joint advantages of geography and technology, the West could scorn all threats. The passing months are changing this situation.

However, politically perhaps more than technologically, London can still pursue an effective policy of dissuasion. Though it occupies a position of major importance in the world, Great Britain does not constitute so decisive an obstacle to world hegemony that enormous risks need to be run to neutralize her. If we were to draw up the balance sheet of advantages and risks in an enterprise of world subjugation, we should no doubt discover that Great Britain's "value" is far from being of the same order as that of the United States. The arsenal of dissuasion America needs is therefore of another dimension than that which would suffice for Great Britain.

And, reasoning by analogy, we can estimate that the instruments of the dissuasion policy of a nation less important than Great Britain may be still more modest. To establish a relation between their number (their destructive power) on the one hand, and on the other the value which the potential aggressor assigns to the nation he wishes to seize, is merely to adopt a rational attitude. This proportionality is written in the facts themselves. Whether it is a question of the pre-atomic era or of the world's new situation since Hiroshima, examples abound of calculations as cautious as they are decisive. We need merely consider certain armed conflicts of the eighteenth

century. But once reason is satisfied and a certain relation has been discovered between the value of the stake
and the extent of the losses incurred in order to seize it,
certain subjective elements intervene which modify the
rigor of such reasoning. No doubt the Third Reich had
its reasons for respecting the integrity of the Swiss national territory. For one thing, it knew that by occupying Switzerland it ran the risk of provoking a strong
national reaction and of creating difficulties for its own
armed forces out of all proportion to Switzerland's strategic and even economic value. But if Switzerland had
compromised the success of the Third Reich's enterprises
by its attitude or had even sided politically with the
Allies, Berlin might have abandoned a "rational" attitude,
accepted the likelihood of a national reaction, and invaded the country anyway. Nevertheless, in the thermonuclear age, a war's balance sheet always shows a singularly heavy "debit" column. Swiss resistance in the
form of guerilla warfare harassing the occupation forces
would have furnished dangers both obvious and easy to
evaluate. To a certain degree, of course, the significance
of such a revolt against the occupying forces could be
minimized, if not concealed from the outer world. But to
suffer the total destruction of three or four major German
cities, to take so obvious a punishment and thereby betray
a victorious Great Nation's vulnerability to the de-
spairing gesture of a conquered nation, no matter how
dearly such a reaction would have to be paid for — this
is a much higher "debit" account than that of the pre-
atomic age. Also, though governments still heed subjective considerations to some extent, it seems that their
dangers are great enough to necessitate a careful calcula-

tion today, and for that calculation to be acted upon. The notion of proportionality between the power of the "deterrent" and the economic, strategic, and political characteristics of the nation determined to use it is a fact. But, of course, what matters is the assessment of the possible aggressive power against which dissuasion must do its work. In this regard, a certain dissemination of the nuclear arsenal is of interest. The knowledge of the laws of atomic strategy accompanies or at least follows the proliferation of this armament where it is being created and tested. So that among the major governments — that is, those which possess nuclear weapons — there exists an increasing similarity of outlook.

Because the evaluation of the risks to be taken is made by leaders who have all learned to calculate according to the same measuring system, a major error of interpretation is less and less plausible and, consequently, the dangers inherent in the policy of dissuasion grow less and less likely. If Americans and Soviets measure the dangers of a recourse to force almost equally and if they attribute similar values to the stake defended by one power and desired by the other, there are few chances that the conflict will break out by accident.

Later on, and on different occasions, we shall examine this new relation between the hierarchy of nations to be subjugated and the quantity of megatons each of them must possess in order to have a better chance to safeguard its freedom. It is easy to list the nations still in the path of Soviet expansionism and it is not impossible, taking them as a function of the advantage their absorption would represent, to classify them by order of increasing importance and to match them with the national forces of dissuasion proportional to their relative importance. Of course, other considerations intervene which would modify this new form of hierarchy. But it is enough that it should exist. If the power of dissuasion at the highest level — that is, the level of the United States — must be absolute, beneath it we may admit degrees in power, and consequently in the dimensions of the various national systems of dissuasion.

Capable of escaping the aggressor's initial assault, of penetrating his defensive network and of dropping enough megatons over his territory, the reprisal forces must also function virtually automatically. To the potential aggressor, reprisal must appear ineluctable. He must be convinced that political and administrative measures have been taken so that, whatever the power and effects of his own first attack, the apparatus of reprisal would, in any case, be set off. This virtual inevitability of reaction, however disturbing it appears, is indispensable. If the adversary did not believe it, he could gamble on the hesitations of his future victim.

In practice, this automatic quality of retaliation can be achieved if a certain number of "danger criteria" — rigorously defined in advance and moreover constantly modified according to the new aspects the threat may assume — serve to release the mechanism of reaction. The adversary must know that once certain hypotheses are verified, certain indications furnished and certain criteria met, the power thus threatened automatically sets in operation the machinery of its reprisal. And it must be widely known that this machinery can respond at top speed. Its "answering time," as the specialists say, must be minimal.

During his press conference of March 4, 1959, President Eisenhower said : " . . . to declare war is a Congressional responsibility . . . but I want to emphasize the fact that when you find yourself placed in a certain situation . . . when the life of the nation is at stake, then time runs out and it's up to the President to decide . . ."

This, in general, is the position of the American government. Of course, the machinery which would pull the atomic trigger remains strictly confidential. And it must be so in order for the policy of dissuasion to achieve its goals.

This new condition of the weapons of dissuasion is the source of much anxiety and the object of many criticisms. It is regarded as the cause of the famous "error" that would unleash a war of annihilation wanted by no one, beginning with the belligerents themselves.

Rigorous integration can limit the dangers of the reprisal machinery and of its speed. But for the nation basing its security on dissuasion, the choice is simple: either this policy of dissuasion fails and the strongest power wins, or else a risk is run in order to give some validity to a concept on which everything depends. It will be objected that weakening the virtues of the policy of dissuasion may be less serious than launching a thermonuclear cataclysm by mistake; particularly since at the rate the threat can now be manifested and materialized, it is easy to make errors in estimation. When ballistic missiles have been substituted for bombers, only an extremely short interval of time remains in which to check the "danger criteria." Before they fall on their targets, ballistic missiles can obviously be destroyed in flight by the nation launching them, but the interval for reconsideration is extremely brief. A procedure like the present

"Fail Safe" system used by the Strategic Air Command bomber crews will no longer be applicable. Today, in case of alert, and if certain indications were furnished to the Strategic Air Command leaders, the atomic bombers would take off at once and head for their targets. But once they had come within a certain distance of the Soviet frontiers or coasts, they would turn back if a new order were not issued to them. Between the alert and the decision to execute the reprisal mission, a certain number of hours would elapse. Generalized use of ballistic missiles is reducing this interval of checking and reconsideration from hours to minutes.

It has been said that a certain number of the future Boeing Minuteman ballistic missiles will be buried in individual silos and that, with these missiles in a constant state of preparedness for launching (stabilization and steering mechanisms in permanent operation), a special firing order could be followed, a few minutes later, by the projection into space of several hundred missiles with atomic warheads — that is, by the departure of an enormous destructive salvo. The intervals of firing and launching would be so short that the Minuteman missiles could easily escape destruction, since they would already be far and high in space when the enemy missiles reached the zone of their launching sites. If the Ballistic Missile Early Warning detection system allows an interval of fifteen minutes, ten of these minutes could still be used for reconsideration, decision, and the transmission of reprisal orders, and the following five for the firing itself. But in this case, the United States government would have to decide to launch its reprisal before aggression was manifest — that is, before the enemy missiles had exploded on

or over American territory. This hypothesis would have
to be included in the defense plans and the corresponding
material organization be set in operation. The prospect
of mutual suicide would have to be considered, and a
government, if not an entire nation, would have to agree
to gamble on such a defense system. This determination
can be subject to guarantees; but the mere fact that technically this possibility of instant reaction exists helps reinforce the policy of dissuasion. It is likely, as a matter of
fact, that no President of the United States would take advantage of the Minuteman missile's capacity for "survival."
But it is possible that, in certain circumstances, Washington may exploit a potential threat of this kind. In such a
case, uncertainty is enough. It obliges discretion and at
least suggests the status quo. And that is what is required
of the policy of dissuasion.

Geography plays a part: it still grants the United
States, today, a considerable advantage over the European
nations. If the U.S.S.R. attacked the United States, its intentions could not remain equivocal for long. An armada
of Russian bombers could not cross the Arctic, the Pacific,
and the Atlantic oceans toward the New World without
setting off a general alert. Given the state of East-West
relations, these flights could not be dismissed as maneuvers or exercises, and there would be mobilization of
defense as of reprisal machinery. As soon as abnormal
echoes appeared on the early warning radar screens, the
Strategic Air Command planes would be launched toward their targets. The American government — that is,
the President of the United States, the National Security
Council, and the Cabinet — would have another three or

four hours before having to make the irremediable decision. In Europe, on the other hand, the NATO radar screens daily register numerous air movements corresponding to planes "grazing" the air space to be defended. If these planes took a "left" or a "right" and headed for the West, the change in direction would be detected only a few minutes before the fall of the bombs. The potential threat is permanent, but because it is permanent and uncertain, it is no longer even a source of anxiety. In any case, the doubt can only be dispelled too late. Tomorrow it will also be less difficult for the radar screens to determine the origin and trajectory of the intercontinental ballistic missiles than to localize offensive short-range projectiles like those that could be launched against targets in Western Europe.

All of which illustrates the close interdependence of the New World and that part of the Old which is to be protected. Nations on either side of the Atlantic benefit from the advantages of geographic distance. Soviet strategic aviation could not destroy, *simultaneously,* airfields and missile-launching sites situated, respectively, in Texas and in Yorkshire without providing Great Britain an alert interval almost as long as that from which the United States would benefit. And if the attacks were not simultaneous, the aggressor would be vulnerable to those reprisal forces he had failed to destroy at their bases.

Now, instead of the present system of collective security, let us consider another. Suppose those European nations capable of constituting a nuclear arsenal were to base their security on a reprisal threat using strictly national means. Facing a Soviet bloc still credited with the same aggressive intentions, dissuasion would no longer be practiced merely by the United States to its own advantage and to that of the entire free world, but by each of these European powers acting separately. The experiment could be made during the next decade and deserves to be considered.

If this were the case, geography would not afford the governments of these nations the same intervals for reconsideration. The "reciprocal alert" from which the NATO nations benefit even today would no longer exist. If the threat were still materialized by bombers, some ten to twenty minutes would separate the detection of these planes from the fall of their missiles. But once ballistic missiles have replaced bombers, the interval will amount to only a few minutes. When dissuasion becomes the security policy of certain European nations, it will impose singular precautions. An erroneous interpretation of Moscow's intentions and even acts is more likely on the European side of the Atlantic; the irremediable gesture of reprisal can be set off only if there is no possible doubt as to the adversary's intentions or actions. When British public opinion was concerned with the dangers of H-bombers flying over Great Britain, Captain B. H. Liddell Hart wrote, in the *New York Herald Tribune,* on January 28, 1958: "In a period of crisis, when passions reach their highest pitch, a world catastrophe could be launched by a few subaltern commands and even by a bomber crew which might assume that the heads of the government or that the allied governments, out of cowardice, were on the point of accepting appeasement at any price." This fear is unjustified, since enough precautions can be taken at every echelon of the political and military hierarchy to minimize such a risk. On the other hand, the

Western European air space is now crossed at such speeds that the launching of the attack and the damages it inflicted would be almost simultaneous.

It follows that the "danger criteria" must be more precise for the safeguarding of Europe than for that of America.

Of course, if the reprisal machinery were set in operation only after the atomic destruction of a certain number of targets, the aggression would be patent and the reaction justified. But in that case, the first shock would have to be "absorbed" — and the reprisal coming only afterwards. It appears that this is the situation of those European nations gambling on a strictly national defense. If the potential aggressor were convinced that by attacking his victim's vital targets first he would not paralyze his victim's reaction; that, even in the chaos of surprise and destruction, the nation thus attacked would nevertheless launch its nuclear reprisal forces; that, in short, by pressing the attack button the aggressor would also pull the reprisal trigger: then the recourse to force must be abandoned and the strategy of dissuasion would have achieved its purposes.

The effectiveness of such a security policy will be inversely proportional to the degree to which its military means depend on public opinion. Can we imagine any Western European nation which, thus attacked, would still unanimously favor an atomic reprisal, even without the risk of incurring dreadful reprisals? Would it not be considered more rational to accept the loss of a few cities and negotiate to save the rest? What would be the good of a nuclear reprisal which could not deprive the adversary of the means of completing his work of destruction? What would be the good of annihilating certain of his cities if, determined to avenge these destructions, he then destroyed the retaliating nation with thermonuclear attacks? Once the policy of dissuasion had failed, reason would demand the shelving of the megatons and the discussion of a new *modus vivendi*. And the greater the disproportion of forces between assailant and victim, the more logical, the more probable the recourse to negotiation.

Considered on these grounds, dissuasion cannot have the slightest influence on a determined adversary. Subordinated to the approval of the members of a government, even to the consent of public opinion, reprisal would be paralyzed. Its probability of adoption would be faint and the aggressor could run the corresponding slight risk. On the other hand, if it were even only plausible that the reprisal would be automatically released if there were an attack, then the assailant would have to accept the corresponding grave risk. Undoubtedly he would abandon the recourse to force.

Another paradox of this period is that the Western democracies must base their security on a policy which would have virtually no meaning if it depended on popular consent. As a consolation, let us point out that it is more a matter of a clockwork mechanism which the Western governments are instituting with the support of public opinion, but whose movement, like that of the hours, escapes all subsequent intervention.

Capable of escaping destruction if its bases were attacked by surprise, conceived to penetrate enemy defenses and organized so that its use is determined automatically, the reprisal force must also represent a sufficient quantity of destruction to be feared by the possible aggressor.

This "sufficient quantity of destruction" is extremely

difficult to ascertain: with regard to thermonuclear destruction, we have, fortunately, little experience, and it is hard to be precise. But this uncertainty increases the risk, counsels discretion, and consequently strengthens the strategy of dissuasion.

Analysis shows that with regard to destruction, everything depends on the nature of the targets chosen by the retaliating power. It is probable that some dozens of missiles or thermonuclear charges would be enough to "collapse" the political and social structure of a major modern and centralized nation. Such destruction, moreover, would have incalculable consequences as to the subsequent capacity of the country thus atomized to take part in world affairs.

It is certain, on the other hand, that in order to destroy a large number of missile-launching sites, both remote and protected by burial underground, enormous quantities of projectiles would be necessary. In 1958, at the end of an exercise intended to study the effect of a thermonuclear attack on the United States, experts concluded that after only twenty-four hours of warfare, America would have lost thirty-six million human lives and would number her wounded above fifty-seven million. The hypotheses concerning the extent of the attack were relatively modest: the population was that of the 1950 census, and less than 300 bombers succeeded in releasing their projectiles. The Soviet planes simultaneously attacked the American airfields (to paralyze reprisal) and the United States cities (to destroy the nation's demographic, industrial, and economic power).

More recently, a similar exercise was organized in behalf of the American civil defense organization. Granted the hypothesis of a thermonuclear attack on the United

States by medium-size Russian air and ballistic forces, it was population damages that were to be ascertained. It was supposed that on a single day in October, 263 thermonuclear bombs or charges, of an average power of some five megatons, were dropped on 224 civilian and military objectives. Seventy-one cities, totaling more than sixty-eight million inhabitants, were attacked by 109 projectiles of a force varying from 1 to 10 megatons and representing a total power of 629 megatons and an average power, per projectile, of 5.5 megatons. The military targets, airfields, launching sites, strategic intersections, etc., "received" 154 projectiles representing a total power of 817 megatons.

Taking into account the anticipated alert conditions, the nature of the terrain and the American social organization, the civil defense exercise showed that for each megaton dropped on the American demographic system a corresponding 70,000 persons were killed, and total losses reached 42 million. Greater New York, for example, was largely destroyed, two 10-megaton projectiles claiming some six million victims there.

Hence, given the present state of American civil defense preparation, and gambling on the slight alert intervals likely in case of an attack made by ballistic missiles, 25 per cent of the population would have vanished and more than half of the American habitat have been destroyed. Over an area constituting approximately 10 per cent of the federal territory, radioactivity would be strong enough to enforce prolonged evacuation whose duration would have to be counted in months and, in certain places, in years. Finally, it would take considerable time to repair material damage, probably ten to twenty years.

Consequently, 300 bombers yesterday, 300 missiles tomorrow, could destroy tens of millions of lives in less than twenty-four hours and represent a quantity of destruction more than sufficient to eliminate America from the concert of nations, at least for many years.

Whether it is aggression or reprisal that aims at the enemy habitat, in either case it would take relatively slight means to produce damages which, whatever the value of the stake, no country could contemplate suffering.

On the other hand, if it were necessary to destroy airfields today and missile-launching sites tomorrow — in short, if it were necessary to attack the opposing reprisal forces — a great number of bombers or missiles would be necessary. The general staffs have conducted studies analogous to those undertaken by the American civil defense services. Less publicized than the civilian studies, the military *Kriegspiele* referred to above have shown that thousands of ballistic missiles would have to be launched in order to destroy several hundred adequately protected missile-launching sites. And even then, in order to prevent a retaliation, these thousands of missiles would have to be launched so that they could crush all the weapons of reprisal at the same time.

And in a few years, when the missile-launching platforms will be mobile and the threatened nation will resort to permanent mobility in order to safeguard its reprisal forces, how can the aggressor discover where to strike? How can his own missile batteries hit targets that make use of a kind of Brownian movement to escape surprise attack?

Let us recall that the victim, on the other hand, cannot retaliate against the aggressor's missile-launching sites. The latter would be empty — at least most of them. The victim would therefore attack the aggressor's large cities. The locations of these targets are known; even at great distances from an air explosion, they are damaged by heat and shock effects and contaminated by radiation. They are necessarily static and cannot be camouflaged or buried underground.

Of course the populations could be evacuated or partially protected. Wohlstetter has calculated that if two 500-kiloton missiles can annihilate 50 per cent of the population of a city of 900,000 inhabitants, its area covering a surface of 100 square kilometers, it would take sixty projectiles of the same power to inflict analogous losses on the same urban population alerted and suitably sheltered. Studying United States vulnerability to thermonuclear warfare, the Rand Corporation[1] has come to the conclusion that if certain protective measures were taken, a nuclear attack of some scope need not lead to total chaos: the American collectivity could retain its structure and its organization. "Simplifying somewhat, one may say that if, during the 1960-1970 period, a carefully prepared general surprise attack were launched, a moderate civil defense program combined with a reasonable military program would be enough to protect with certainty about half the population, and with less predictability another quarter, the fate of the last quarter remaining uncertain," Rand's H. Kahn wrote in the *Bulletin of the Atomic Scientists* for January 1959.

Obviously expecting a certain reaction from his victim, the aggressor would empty his own major urban centers of most of their populations and do his utmost to minimize the effects of reprisal. He would nevertheless have

[1] *Report on a Study of Non-Military Defense*, R. 322-RC, July 1, 1958.

to act quickly and adhere to arrangements that could be effected in a few hours, for his offensive strategy could succeed only if it retained the advantage of surprise. Otherwise, how overtake the missiles he wished to destroy at their launching sites? Consequently, it would be dangerous for the aggressor to evacuate his cities in advance, thereby sounding the alarm.

But even if, according to the Rand estimate, most of the inhabitants were to escape death, they would find their cities in ruins, their territory largely contaminated and in places completely uninhabitable, their possessions annihilated. The conditions of modern life would have disappeared. An enormous reconstruction program would have to be instituted in order to achieve, after many years' effort, a level of life analogous to that which existed on the eve of the thermonuclear exchange.

Atomic aggression would have to grant the nation intending to employ it considerable advantages if they must be paid for at such a price.

This is why, once directed against the adversary's demographic system, the threat of thermonuclear reprisal assumes its complete significance and acquires a real dissuasive force. The easier it is for the potential victim to materialize this threat, the more the potential aggressor is likely to believe that it will be used. And in the age of ballistic missiles with thermonuclear charges, the targets constituted by the habitat remain all the easier to annihilate.

Determinedly peaceful, anticipating the use of force only if obliged to resort to it, the nation adopting the policy of dissuasion must take not its aggressor's armed forces but its civilian population as its target. And in order for its defensive strategy to have any validity, everyone must be aware that in case of need it would direct its reprisal against the assailant's urban centers. Another paradox: the assailant would be led to attack his victim's reprisal forces — that is, his strictly military targets — first, while the peaceful nation, though attacked, would have no other recourse than to raze the enemy urban centers.

Eager to find a moral basis for the possible use of weapons of massive destruction, certain authors[1] have supported the notion of "proportional dissuasion." The West would use atomic weapons of low and medium power, if necessary, on the field of battle, but its high-power A- and H-explosives would be launched against nonmilitary objectives only if the aggressor proceeded to a generalized and indiscriminate attack.

The Pentagon never agreed to subscribe to such limitations. Since there had long been a difference of scale between the most powerful chemical weapons and the least powerful atomic weapons, it may have feared that by accepting the principle of proportional dissuasion the West might weaken its position instead of reinforcing it. Hesitating to resort to its medium-caliber atomic arsenal, it might encourage the adversary to exploit the formula of localized conflicts. And if such conflicts assumed a serious character, the West would deprive itself of the advantage of intimidation, for the East would know that its own really vulnerable targets were safe (this was the case with regard to the Chinese air bases beyond the Yalu during the Korean war, though at the time the Western self-constraint applied only to conventional explosives). Moreover, experience shows that with regard to the poli-

[1] "On Limiting Atomic War," Rear Admiral Sir Anthony Buzzard.

tical use of nuclear weapons, a widely publicized but
vague determination is more valuable than specific promises that cannot always be kept and that would furnish the
other side valuable indications as to the policy the latter
could pursue with impunity.

The development and imminent generalization of low-
power atomic weapons gives a new interest to the notion
of proportional dissuasion. Naturally, if the stake were
important and if the aggressor were trying to seize it by
an all-out attack, no limitation need be observed. Either a
nation possessing a ballistic and nuclear arsenal is threatened and does not hesitate to destroy its enemy's great
urban centers, or else the dispute is purely marginal.[1] In
the latter case, it must be understood that the atomic
weapons of increasing power would be used until the adversary either came to terms or was reduced to the preceding case, risking the destruction of both population
and habitat.

Great Britain, for instance, has no choice. The nature
and importance of the nuclear forces it can wield would
limit the targets of its reprisal forces to large urban centers. There can be no question of the Bomber Command's
attacking enemy armed forces or preparing a counterbattery with its missiles. The threat would not be taken
seriously, because a nation like Great Britain does not
possess the means of materializing it. The defense policy
implicitly contained in the famous White Paper of 1957
answers the imperatives of the thermonuclear age: it in-
forms the world that aggression against Great Britain
would cost more than it would yield.

----

[1] By "marginal" we mean here a conflict in which the nuclear powers are
not directly engaged. For them, the struggle is marginal, though its character could be vital for the nation which would be its stake.

This defense policy poses problems of conscience which British public opinion has been concerned with for years. During the Second World War, the strategic bombardment of the Third Reich was not exactly approved by the British government, but it was nevertheless pursued to the last days of the war. Today, the strategy of "deterrence" is loudly criticized, but since no alternative exists, it will be condemned by morality but reinforced by the facts.

When a nation the size of Great Britain is led to practice dissuasion with regard to a power like the U.S.S.R., the threat of reprisal can affect only the targets Britain can reach — that is, the Soviet population itself. Inadmissible in the Western context, the fact remains. It is not necessary, moreover, that London make its intentions explicit. There need be only a certain likelihood that the Bomber Command will attack the Soviet urban centers for London's strategy of dissuasion to assume its full significance with regard to Moscow.

If the threat of British reprisal affects the opposing habitat, it is not necessary for the Bomber Command to be able to inflict damages as extensive as those the American Strategic Air Command must be capable of. The thermonuclear force can be proportional to the value of the stake it is defending. Naturally, the value of this stake is fixed by the potential aggressor, and it is on the latter's estimate, however subjective and tentatively known this is, that the nature and power of an effective dissuasion force will depend. It is obvious that in the age of nuclear explosives, the dangers of violence or the threat of violence are so great that the risks run must be constantly compared to the value of the goals violence is intended to achieve.

In so far as these values are measurable, a scale of the destructive powers of the various forces of national dissuasion should be calibrated with the hierarchy of nations as determined by the aggressor nation. If Wohlstetter estimates that under certain conditions the U.S.S.R. would be willing to lose twenty million men in order to erase the United States from the map, analogous speculation suggests that Great Britain could discourage any threat if her Bomber Command were capable of inflicting ravages equivalent to a fourth or a fifth of the figure advanced for the United States. And, as we have said, Switzerland or Denmark, in the same strategic and political circumstances, would have the privilege of imposing respect on still better terms — for instance, if one of these nations were credited with a reprisal force capable of destroying only two or three cities and of annihilating less than a half-million inhabitants.

Carefully evaluating this kind of risk, the Soviets might calculate not only the dangers of a possible reaction of a force numerically as low as that of the British Bomber Command, but would also take a third party into account — in today's terms, an American intervention.

If there were to be a dispute and subsequently an exchange of attacks between the U.S.S.R. and Great Britain, it is possible that the incident would remain limited to these two nations. But it is just as likely that the British reaction would involve the Strategic Air Command. Indirectly threatened, Washington would support London. Or the United States might even seize the occasion to settle the fate of its sole and powerful adversary once and for all.

This notion of a chain reaction starting with a first exchange of attacks possibly helped determine the nuclear program prepared by the British general staff. A pact is exposed to too many dangers; under the pressure of circumstances, the obligations of a treaty may not be binding. On the other hand, London might well calculate that if the Bomber Command were sent into action and English atom bombs dropped on Soviet targets in reprisal for a similar Russian attack, there would be a good chance that America would follow suit.

Is the hypothesis likely enough for the Soviets to consider it? Intended to be merely the percussion cap of a terrible exchange of attacks, the dissuasion potential of a nation like Great Britain could indeed be fearful, though limited to only a few nuclear weapons. The weapon of the weak, the small atomic arsenal would lead to the use of a large one and to the confrontation of the major powers.

In France, too, this notion has been advanced to justify French military atomic policy and the concept of security based on a necessarily modest nuclear arsenal.

For some ten years, this ingenious means of defense has maintained its value. Today some contest its advantage, pointing out that since the United States itself is vulnerable to Soviet ballistic missiles, the automatic nature of American intervention is less certain. If, therefore, America were to come to the support of a friendly nation, she would be placed in a difficult situation from a military point of view. She would either have to destroy her adversary's reprisal forces — and such an operation would be all the less feasible because these forces, long since alerted, would be protected by underground storage or mobility — or else suffer their terrible effects. To annihilate the Soviet cities would present no operational difficulties but would not paralyze the Soviet reprisal, which would be launched at once. Threatened with enormous damages if she were to come to the aid of Great Britain, America might hesitate. And once the likelihood of American intervention was in doubt, the U.S.S.R. would recover a share of its freedom of action with regard to the United Kingdom.

It is, in fact, plausible for the potential aggressor to make the following calculation: if seriously threatened a powerful adversary would probably use his megatons of destruction in retaliation. But in a question of intervening for the sake of *another* country, even a friendly power, hesitation is particularly likely, for the laws of nuclear strategy are unfavorable to such intervention.

It is therefore not certain that the minor atomic arsenal of the secondary nations can function effectively as a wick to ignite the major powers' powder keg. This form of security is not automatic. It will be all the less so when missiles assume a larger strategic importance and every power will be exposed to their ravages. A certain proportion subsists between a nation's importance and the nuclear armament it needs in order to practice a strategy of dissuasion successfully. But the "wick" policy, if dangerous, may also turn out to be extremely disappointing for those who decide to depend on it. If a nuclear power intends to base its security on dissuasion, it is essential that the forces at its disposal fulfill a certain number of technological conditions, chiefly that the "quantity of destruction" applicable to the wealth and demographic system of its possible assailant be large enough to prejudice the latter against aggression. Even in the thermonuclear age, when a few missiles are enough to inflict great damages, security cannot be obtained cheaply. It is more difficult than ever to find a partner ready to deal such blows — and consequently to receive them — in another's stead.

Here too, these statements are subject to modification. The risk to the aggressor of provoking the Strategic Air Command could be of such gravity that American nonintervention must be absolutely certain. Up to now Washington's reactions have shown the Soviets that they cannot gamble on American nonintervention, although the stakes have been relatively minor and United States security has not been directly threatened. The "wick" policy therefore retains a meaning, at least as an "accelerator" in the spiral toward the showdown. Yet despite the advantages it can still confer on certain nations, such a policy is singularly disturbing for others. It is regarded in America as superfluous, costly, full of risks; beyond the iron curtain it is considered eminently dangerous.

For the military means of a strategy of dissuasion to assume any value, many conditions must be fulfilled.

Nuclear explosives and carrying vehicles — planes or missiles — must survive the first attacks of an aggressor who has the advantage of surprise and, of course, the superiority of power and initiative. Next, this reprisal force — if it consists of bombers — must penetrate the aggressor's defenses. The reprisal must be set off automatically, so that the possible aggressor knows that neither political subjection, moral constraint, nor fear of additional punishment can paralyze it. Finally, the nature and number of the reprisal's targets must be proportional to its means. It is essential that the quantity of destruction which the reprisal force still represents when it reaches its targets annihilate at least those advantages the aggressor counted on gaining from his attack. Of course, what matters is that the aggressor nation — or rather its government — reach these conclusions.

If this were to be the case, the first of the two terms of the product characterizing the policy of dissuasion would be distinctly positive. There remains the second term of this product — that is, the intention to use, if need be, a technologically valid reprisal force, or at least one regarded as such by the adversary.

The Reluctance to Offer Reprisal

At the cost of many billions of dollars, and by exhausting all the recourses of science and technology, the Strategic Air Command has been set in operation. Its leader knows that it can annihilate a continent and that its power of intimidation forces the enormous Soviet army to remain inactive. But if certain conditions were fulfilled — if, for instance, the danger criteria defined by the Strategic Air Command's operation plans were to be met, would the thermonuclear reprisal really be launched? If there were a determination to make a nation's security and the defense of its way of life depend on the launching of such forces of destruction, would this determination, however easy to carry out, actually be realized? In order to take into account the peculiar logic of dissuasion, the question must be put as follows: is it likely that a government, even if it were placed in a critical situation, would take the responsibility of exterminating a vast population? As for the aggressor, where does he locate the "ignition point" of a thermonuclear war? How far must he go to provoke such a reaction, and above all, how far could he go *without* provoking this reaction?

As long as America had both the monopoly of the new explosive and that of the carrying vehicle, such questions were of interest only because of the moral constraints which the Western nations, and the United States in particular, imposed upon themselves.

These constraints were already being discussed by the Western powers at the time of the Korean conflict. An atomic attack on the U.S.S.R. was not seriously contemplated, of course, but the use of nuclear explosives against the targets of the Korean peninsula, even against those beyond the Yalu, was certainly studied. The conditions under which the conflict developed, the precedent of Hiroshima, the political atmosphere of the moment, and also the nature of the atomic stockpile then available to the United States were so many reasons for fighting only with "conventional" weapons. However serious and costly, the conflict did not justify the use of such a destructive force. Already surprised by its own determination to resist, the Western world could not, further, cross the atomic threshold and create another Hiroshima.

Four years later, when Dien Bien Phu was besieged, the West again considered using the atomic weapon. This time, too, the struggle was not proportional to a nuclear intervention on Asiatic soil. Further, monopoly of the explosive had been lost, and public opinion feared an extension of the conflict and even envisaged an all-out war originating in Indochina. This was to be completely ignorant of the relation of then-existing forces and to hold cheap the close relation of risk to stake in every conflict. But public opinion cannot be asked to make such calculations.

In 1958, four years after Dien Bien Phu, it was not a question of setting the Strategic Air Command in operation, but merely of authorizing the American fleet to use the best weapons available to maintain the status quo in the China Sea. And behind these weapons loomed others, omnipotent ones. Thanks to Mr. Dulles' determination, Peking retreated. The stake of the conflict — the islands of Quemoy and Matsu — seemed to Peking out of proportion to the risk that would have to be run to test the Secretary of State's intentions.

These three stages of the East-West struggle have been reviewed here because they illustrate the share of political determination in the effectiveness of dissuasion. In military terms, the atomic monopoly facilitated the expression of such determination in 1950, even in 1954, much more in 1958, at which date Mr. Dulles' determination, however, offset and even outbid the nuclear parity the Soviets had achieved.

These three conflicts were secondary in so far as they could not justify the operation of the Strategic Air Command. The American atomic bombers played the role of a reserve force which would have been invoked if the struggle had exceeded certain limits and aimed at other goals. But since the Korean conflict, technological development has permitted a "descent" in the scale of destructive power, and consequently the possible use of the new weapons in the course of minor shows of force. Defense Secretary Neil McElroy emphasized this once again, after Messrs. Wilson and Quarles, when on June 13, 1958, he declared to the press: "Atom bombs — 'clean' ones, I hope — of limited power will be used by the United States during any 'small war' on condition that it is to our advantage to use them."

The question is whether America, its security threatened, would actually launch its bombers and missiles against the U.S.S.R. Since the entire political and military machinery permits such a reaction to be virtually automatic, the answer is obviously affirmative.

Can such a determination be a lasting one? Once the American people is aware of its territory's vulnerability and realizes that its reprisals could multiply tenfold the devastation of an enemy attack that was intended to intimidate its leaders or neutralize its strategic weapons, will it still subscribe to the policy of "deterrence"? But doesn't the American people already know — hasn't it known for a long time, and indeed before it was true — that it is vulnerable to a Soviet thermonuclear attack? Whether in regard to financing armament programs or organizing huge passive defense exercises, public officials have been warning the American people for years of the dangers threatening it. Yet Washington has not modified its policy and yielded to adverse pressures. Korea, Formosa, Lebanon, and Jordan have been so many "affairs," "incidents" which bear witness to American serenity in facing the revolution in strategy. Provided the American people believes its cause to be just, it will accept enormous risks for a long time to come. Yet since it has emerged from the state of security in which its geography has kept it throughout its entire history, the American people must eventually provide a more complicated answer than the one it offers today to the question of the validity of its policy of dissuasion.

Moreover, if instead of being certain and ineluctable, it

were merely likely, the American reprisal would not lose its power of intimidation. This is the advantage conferred by power: it makes provocation worthless, even indirect provocation. The Strategic Air Command bombers — and the first ballistic missiles replacing them — represent so powerful an annihilation potential that even if the probability were extremely slight of setting such a destructive force in operation, the corresponding risk, however tenuous, is one that could not be taken.

But when a nation such as Great Britain uses dissuasion against the U.S.S.R., the disparity of forces necessarily influences British determination and, consequently, limits the fear such a policy must inspire to be fully effective. If London, threatened by Moscow, were to take a stand and succeed in making its reprisal feared, it would succeed in imposing the status quo. The threat of aggression or even an ultimatum would be avoided and Moscow would have to abandon the use of violence against Great Britain. But if the U.S.S.R. went a step further, if it gambled on the fear it could inspire or on a certain apathy in the British government which would make it prefer negotiation to combat, or even if it were to agree to "absorb" the shock of the English reprisal and penalize its victim later, this would certainly be a defeat for Great Britain and would perhaps mean annihilation as well.

Differing from Washington, London estimates that the destruction would be unequal and unequally endured. Despite its determination, despite its atomic panoply, the British people could not confront the possible aggressor with the henceforth classical dilemma: the status quo or a cataclysm fatal to both belligerents.

Yet materially, it is easier for Great Britain than for the

United States to adopt a strategy of dissuasion. Though less powerful than the American weapons, her instruments are nevertheless capable of protecting Great Britain. We know that with regard to destruction and suffering, the U.S.S.R. could not "accept" from Great Britain what it would be willing to pay to annihilate the United States for good. In military terms, the logic of dissuasion requires that the inequality of forces not condemn the weaker side. Politically, on the other hand, this inequality further weakens the weaker side. This is because uninitiated public opinion does not yet understand that in the age of the atom, numerical superiority is no longer omnipotent. If it is furnished with nuclear weapons and appears determined to wield them rather than to yield, the weaker side can still protect its independence and assure the integrity of its territory. But it is not generally obvious that such a thing is possible. The government of a threatened democratic nation would have considerable difficulty publicizing a resolution which must be firm in direct proportion to the inferiority of its forces.

If we were to analyze the validity of the dissuasion policy pursued by the United States and Great Britain — and tomorrow by France — we must admit that the weight of public opinion is all the more significant the greater — or the greater appears — the margin of Soviet superiority. The paralysis factor of public opinion would no doubt be less decisive in the case of a U.S.A.-U.S.S.R. conflict than in the hypothesis of a serious dispute between Great Britain and the Soviet Union: by offering provocation to the Strategic Air Command, the U.S.S.R. would be risking more than by opposing the English Bomber Command. And during this kind of poker game that pressures enemy public opinion to force its government to yield, intimidation is less dangerous in regard to London than to Washington.

The second term of the product schematizing the strategy of dissuasion seems, as we see, much more uncertain than the first. Technology and economy, one buttressing the other, suffice to create a "retaliation force" inspiring fear and capable of outlawing force. But the determination to use such means depends in large measure on the support of public opinion. The latter, necessarily subjective, is at the mercy of every alarm, sensitive to every threat, even those that cannot be materialized.

It follows that the democracies cannot pursue a strategy of dissuasion save in the service of an absolutely vital cause. The independence, the very life of a democracy would have to be directly threatened for a recourse to its nuclear weapons to seem legitimate, for reprisal to be plausible and consequently feared.

After the Suez incident, a brilliant polemicist wrote that the failure of the United Kingdom's defense policy was patent, since its atomic weapons had not kept Mr. Khrushchev from issuing his famous warning. He thereby inferred that it was better for France to abandon a costly form of armament whose uselessness had just been so clearly demonstrated.

This was to be ignorant of the area in which the nuclear explosive can be effective and at the same time to bring an extremely summary judgment to bear on the British defense policy. It was obvious that during the Suez incident — which had furthermore divided public opinion and the British Parliament — the Bomber Command's atomic missiles could not be used against either Moscow or Cairo. The stake was far too minor for London to contemplate —

however briefly — setting up an atomic scarecrow, particularly one limited to high- and medium-power explosive charges. Mr. Khrushchev was free to launch his skillful allusion to the atomization of London and Paris. In the case in point, the ignorance, division, and even the stupidity of the Western camp invited boldness. How amused Moscow must have been when London and Paris found in Mr. Khrushchev's phrases a threat the Soviet leader had not dared put there.

By subscribing to the creation of a reprisal force, the British government did not intend to supply its nation with a means of intimidation currently utilizable on the international scene. Aside from the political advantages from which the nation becoming the third atomic power would benefit, it was attempting to dispel any threat to Britain's very foundations. The thermonuclear weapons have no significance save in such a hypothesis.

If, for instance, in November 1956, the Hungarian government had possessed the means to inflict only three "Hiroshimas" on the U.S.S.R., it is probable that the fear of such a retaliation would have imposed negotiation and a new *modus vivendi* between Budapest and Moscow, and that neither repression nor occupation would have occurred. An atomic reaction would appear plausible only in facing a threat like that of the Soviet divisions which invaded Hungary. The greater the disparity of forces, the more critical the situation of the threatened nation would have to be, so that recourse to the nuclear arsenal would not appear irrational. And if such a reaction seemed likely to the aggressor, the latter would modify his plans and abandon force in order not to provoke its use against himself.

As a weapon of despair, nuclear retaliation would have

only an extremely limited field of political action. On
April 21, 1959, speaking before the Senate Foreign Affairs
Committee, the new American Secretary of State, Mr.
Christian Herter, was questioned by Senator Morse:
". . . Don't you think that some kind of agreement is
necessary between the President and the representatives
of the people . . . so that the conflicts which risk drag-
ging humanity into a generalized atomic war would be at
least discussed in Congress . . . especially since once involved in such a war, we would be led to use our atomic
bombs and our hydrogen bombs." To which the Secretary
of State replied: "I don't know what kind of agreement
you're referring to . . . Coming back to the question
of the behavior of the men in charge, I cannot imagine
that the President of the United States would lead us
into a generalized atomic war unless we ourselves were in
danger or unless preparations had actually been made to
destroy us." No sooner was it in print than this phrase became the object of many commentaries. Interpreted as applying only to the United States, Mr. Herter's words limited the policy of dissuasion to the protection of American
territory. It is no doubt in this sense, thinking as a good
demagogue, that Senator Morse understood it. As it
happens, the Secretary of State was referring to the entire
free world and more particularly those nations whose
safety the United States was guaranteeing by treaty.
"Ourselves" was, among other things, the Western community under the protection of the American "deterrent."

But it is difficult to rally a Congress, a Parliament, or
public opinion to a policy of dissuasion which could
nevertheless be pursued, without running excessive risks,
to the advantage of a large community of allied states.

Inhibited by its fears, Western public opinion took the opposite view and by pressuring its governments spoiled a defensive position which in fact was quite impregnable.

On this side of the world, in varying degrees according to the nations involved, popular support can result only from an enormous effort of propaganda and explanation, or from an intuitive grasp, on the part of the masses of people, of extremely complex scientific and technological phenomena with many political consequences. The democratic governments find it difficult to justify their actions, and the people are no more apt to grasp the numerous implications of the nuclear fact. Actually, the more enlightened public opinion seems, the more it burdens its governments and the less the latter are free to act and to exploit their specialists' achievements. The public meetings in Trafalgar Square have not been forgotten, nor the parades and protest marches that broke out in Great Britain when a part of the population rose against its government's nuclear policy. The contrast is striking between the ideas set forth by the experts in the White Paper on Defense in 1959, and the notions advanced by the Labor opposition, the trade unions, and a considerable part of the English intelligentsia. The former, provided with all the available information, have pondered the new security conditions, whereas the latter base their position on the lessons of the past, on frequently oversimplified deductions, and on a subjective argument easily followed by the majority of public opinion.

How could it be otherwise, in such circumstances, when the statesman, the scientist, and the "savant" have so often shown themselves incapable of disentangling the threads of the nuclear skein? When on December 14, 1951, Mr.

Finletter, then Secretary of the Air Force, declared "that the bombing of the Communist bases beyond the Yalu . . . would lead to the most horrible attacks of man against man and also to the third world war," did he really suppose that, without nuclear weapons, the Sino-Soviet forces would have joined battle against an adversary abundantly furnished with them? In April 1957, Pius XII sent the Japanese Prime Minister a text containing the following phrases: "Each power seeks to outstrip the other by the mounting and unfortunately real terrors imposed on it. Instead of this futile waste of scientific activity, of effort and material means which the preparation of this catastrophe costs . . . the wise men of every nation and every faith must feel the serious moral obligation to pursue the noble goal of mastering these energies in the service of mankind."

No doubt the Sovereign Pontiff could scarcely say anything else to the Prime Minister of Japan. But was it any use? Was it even true? "This futile waste of scientific activity" is nevertheless of a nature to prolong the existence of a privileged though minority-controlled world on which the Church itself depends, whether it wishes to or not. There is no question of fighting with the help of this nuclear arsenal, but of prolonging the status quo by discouraging aggression and outlawing the use of force. It is not certain that morality contradicts such an attitude. Moreover, no alternative exists.

In Oslo, Doctor Schweitzer demanded that the nuclear tests be halted, and in Bonn, Professor von Weizsäcker, speaker for a group of eighteen scientists, violently attacked Chancellor Adenauer, whom he censured for planning to equip the German forces with American atomic weapons. On May 10, 1957, assuming it was replying to the wishes of public opinion, the Bundestag asked for "a world-wide disarmament, outlawing weapons of massive destruction and authorizing the halt of experimental nuclear explosions." None of the authors of these protests seems to have considered the providential character of a weapon capable of offsetting the West's numerical inferiority. Nor has any of them understood that an attitude such as theirs weakens the virtues of a policy of dissuasion which nevertheless deserves their support, since it protects the minority by imposing peace.

On March 10, 1958, an appeal to the "struggle against atomic death" was issued by a group of German notables, among them Erich Ollenhauer, Carlo Schmid, Heinemann, Pastor Niemöller, and Nobel Prize-winner Max Born: ". . . the race for nuclear weapons and the installation of launching platforms on German territory can only increase the danger . . . The Bundestag must support the plans to create a de-nuclearized zone . . ." These declarations, made by eminent and celebrated men, are nevertheless without any scientific, strategic, or political basis. To establish a non-nuclear zone on either side of the present iron curtain would oblige the departure of the very American troops which, in the present relation of East-West forces, can neutralize Soviet numerical superiority only by the threat of using atomic weapons. "Disengagement" would weaken the policy of dissuasion pursued by America to the advantage of Western Europe and would facilitate the Soviet strategy. From England, Bertrand Russell wrote, in the *New York Herald Tribune* for January 4, 1958: "It is an unimaginable folly to suppose that the manufacture of the hydrogen bomb increases the security of our country." But a few lines later, the British scientist contradicted himself as follows: "Mr. Khrushchev emphasizes the destruction Soviet bombs could inflict upon Great Britain. He seems to have forgotten that the prevailing winds, in Europe, blow from the West and that the fallout from Soviet bombs dropped on Great Britain would probably have disastrous effects on Russia." [1] This was to recognize the meaninglessness of the recourse to force, because of the existence of nuclear weapons and not because they had been banned. As for "disengagement," after Mr. Kennan spoke on the BBC, it was Air Marshal Sir John Slessor who wrote that the twenty Western divisions could not prevent the outbreak of localized conflicts in Europe, since "they could not defend themselves against forces three times more powerful." Which would be true only if, once some forty divisions were at grips in Europe, the West renounced its weapons of massive destruction.

These fears, these inadequate arguments, and these incomplete deductions do not stand up under the close scrutiny security matters deserve in the nuclear age. But by the attraction they exert upon public opinion, by reason of their very facility, they pose the real question of the survival of the Western bloc. Provided with every material means of gaining time and capable, behind its atomic rampart, of gradually raising the world's standard

[1] Lord Russell's argument is moreover incorrect in military and scientific terms. Only a few high-altitude explosions could devastate the British Isles — too few for the radioactive fallout to be so dangerous. On the other hand, if Great Britain, contrary to Lord Russell's wishes, possessed ballistic missiles with nuclear charges, the Russian bombs or missiles would have to explode near the ground in order to neutralize them. Millions of tons of radioactive waste would then be projected into space, and Lord Russell's thesis might be at least partially verified.

of living, the West is continually undermining the foundations of its own security.

In December 1950, when UN forces were fighting in Korea, the question arose of discovering whether the intensive bombardment of the enemy's rear lines would force the communists to retreat across the Yalu. A major French newspaper wrote at the time: ". . . There remains the use of the A-bomb. Because it was decisive against Japan, some overwrought minds suppose that it would soon bring China to terms . . . This means committing in cold blood a massacre which the Chinese masses would doubtless absorb readily enough . . . It means sending through all of Europe a shudder of horror which Soviet propaganda will doubtless be able to utilize. And who knows if the U.S.S.R. itself will not select this moment to stake her all and answer the European challenge . . . The most willful cynicism collapses before such evidence." The author of these words was forgetting that the first Soviet atomic explosion was only fifteen months old at the time, and that the disparity of atomic stockpiles granted the West every advantage. He was also unaware that if the use of atomic weapons had been even likely, North Korea would have abandoned its invasion plans. Such were the fears and scruples expressed by the article quoted above which limited the likelihood of an atomic intervention and which as a consequence directly invited aggression by giving the heavy battalions their obvious advantage over the light ones.

The world in general has not yet grasped the nature and meaning of the military, and consequently political, upheavals resulting from the fission and fusion of the atom. British public opinion, for instance, appears to be divided even on the question of insuring its own security. One can imagine a nation whose independence would be guaranteed by a nuclear power and which would prefer to renounce this form of security rather than risk — even to its own exclusive benefit — pursuing the strategy of dissuasion with the aid of atomic weapons. On May 6, 1954 — that is, on the eve of the fall of Dien Bien Phu — M. Christian Pineau declared at the French Assembly: ". . . My dear colleagues, we shall not be tempted by the mirage of an intervention which may or may not save the Dien Bien Phu garrison, but which would bring war down on our heads again and risk spreading it over the entire world." (Applause from the Left.) Such an intervention was what, at the request of Monsieur Bidault, then Minister of Foreign Affairs, the American government had at least contemplated, and which the *Journal Officiel* of June 9, 1954, refers to as follows: ". . . a plan of American intervention was, at our request, not only under study but in preparation and virtually in the process of execution. The American press, better informed about matters that concern us than the French Parliament itself, has revealed that the American intervention at Dien Bien Phu was to have occurred on April 28, that the boats were on the way, loaded with atomic weapons, and that President Eisenhower was to ask Congress for the necessary authorization on April 26 . . ."

This time, on May 6, 1954, it was a representative of the nation which would have benefited from the American intervention who objected to such assistance. To believe for a moment that, in the contemporary context and taking into account the relation of the existing forces, Dien Bien Phu would have set off a war which would subsequently have "spread over the entire world," was to be completely unaware of the rules to which East-West conflict have been subject since Hiroshima. The risk of provoking such a general conflagration was much smaller in 1954, when it was a question of saving the doomed garrison, that in 1958, when Mr. Dulles performed an analogous maneuver for the sake of Quemoy and Formosa. Of course in April 1954, London put pressure on Washington to abandon Dien Bien Phu to its fate, but a large share of French public opinion, ill informed of the new laws of strategy, took fright and, indirectly, capitulated. And the negotiation policy pursued in Geneva immediately afterward had the majority of the country behind it.

The reaction of French public opinion is virtually that of the whole of Western public opinion. Although it has been the only one possible, Mr. Dulles' policy has not been supported by the West. It took many months for the consequences of the Secretary of State's death to be realized. Only a few groups of specialists have grasped the spirit and use of the new laws which determine the political and military strategy of the atom, and realize that they must base their reasoning on unfamiliar concepts and permanently subscribe to apparent paradoxes. Therefore the initiates see no means of taking the public into their confidence. It is for such reasons that the policy of dissuasion is so badly misunderstood — often even by those who are led to pursue it — that it is no easier to win public opinion over to its demands than it is to inform it of its possibilities.

Gambling on these misunderstandings, the adversary has no difficulty intervening in Western affairs by opposing the leaders to the led. It is enough for the former to evince a certain firmness for the latter to grow frightened and demand appeasements and concessions.

Once the Western governments attempt to express public opinion without having documented it beforehand, they run considerable risk of leading both their country and the democracy they imagine they are defending to their destruction. The complexity of the problems posed by the two systems confronting each other today is not always within the grasp of an average understanding. It must be admitted, moreover, that with regard to questions of defense, incomprehension is much more frequently the product of scientific and intellectual circles than a characteristic of the man in the street, for the latter is generaly absorbed by quite other concerns.

Though quite different from each other, both as to their cause and their object, the violent incidents that have occurred in Turkey, in Korea, and Japan are due, in large measure, to public incomprehension of today's problems.

Obviously we are living through a period characterized by scientific and technological achievements which, by their complexity as by their too-rapid development, escape both the specialized technician in his particular discipline and the man in the street. Either the latter's social condition does not yet permit him to form the slightest judgment on international or even national problems, or, on the contrary, the interest awakened by a certain prosperity leads him to concern himself only with his personal affairs — but in either case, the way is initially clear for administrations or rulers. In the socially and economically underdeveloped countries, there are not yet "citizens," and in the others, there are none left. In both groups, the problems of international and national life appear too complicated. This indifference of public opinion to public matters, wherever manifested, is not without danger. In certain circumstances and under certain influences, public opinion can be made sensitive to the governmental action it was previously unaware of, and then mobilized against it.

The study and conduct of public affairs are increasingly the task of the technician rather than of the politician or statesman. Prepared for their task, furnished with information to which the public has no access, specializing in the analysis of questions relating to their disciplines, these technicians form an omnipotent administration. By definition, one might say — and also by organization — this administration has the greatest probability of seeing clearly.

It is therefore natural that the political context of world affairs be minimized and that the technocracy take over. In one sense, the phenomenon is not a new one. It is a fact of long standing that in most of the Western democracies the opposition's arguments are more emotional than rational, and that it is difficult for the opposition to gain ascendancy over the arguments of a government informed by its administration. Most often, moreover, once the party that was formerly the opposition is in office, it pursues a policy quite close to that of the government it criticized when it was concerned to replace it. Everything occurs as if there were no longer any choice among several policies — as if there were, indeed, only one: that which results from the deeper study of questions and consequently that which the administration is obliged to endorse.

The practice of democracy, as it is conceived in Western Europe, is therefore less and less easy. Each drifts in opposite directions: the administrated population toward the satisfaction of individual destinies, and the government toward the conduct of affairs complex enough to interest only itself and its specialists. Without checks, power leads to excesses. Consequently, it will be difficult to establish a *modus vivendi* on such bases. The events that occurred in Turkey and in the Middle East during the spring of 1960 have revealed the force of an opposition with new causes, since despite difficult material circumstances it attacked the foreign or domestic policy of the incriminated governments more than their wage and salary policy or their social action. Another characteristic of such opposition movements is that the student class has played a decisive role in them. In other words, considering the political conditions which existed in Korea, in Turkey, or in Japan, the students were perhaps the only group able to oppose their government's action. The education of these young men predisposed them to judge, to discuss, and consequently to contest the bases of a policy whose justifications they could not grasp, lacking as they did the necessary data and never having been informed of the reasons for governmental action. Not yet sharing their elders' concerns and responsibilities, they were free to run out into the streets and make demonstrations. Their youth did the rest.

The eruption of young people into the political and administrative life of Korea, Turkey, or Japan has been all the more violent in that there existed, in these nations, no check to their intervention. Between the sovereign state — remote, misunderstood, and as inaccessible as

Kafka's castle — and a resigned or indifferent people, there could be — aside from the army, in Turkey and Korea — no other group of functioning collectivity capable of commitment and concern.

The example will no doubt be followed. We must expect more and more intervention from student groups or from the pressure armies can exert on the governments — when they do not constitute the governments themselves. This is the corollary of the increasing technical nature of public affairs.

During the incidents of 1960 in the Middle and Far East, the status quo with regard to security was not modified in Korea or in Turkey, at least in immediate terms. In Japan, on the other hand, it was precisely the security policy which was aimed at — particularly since there was no alternative offered, and since Japan, like other nations, had no choice save between a commitment to the United States, with all its risks — and isolation, with all its dangers.

But how obtain the support of the Japanese people — and even of its intelligentsia — when it is a matter of inducing that people to share the risks of a defense policy based on a possible recourse to atomic weapons? Nowhere are the apparent paradoxes to the nuclear age commonly accepted. It is difficult to get "everyone" to understand that the technology of armaments has reached such results, that — at present at least — it is no longer possible to base a strictly defensive policy on a defensive doctrine and defensive weapons. This evidence is not generally admitted, and less in Japan than elsewhere. No one is prepared to believe that by threatening a destruction which could be beyond the value of the most coveted prize, the new weapons impose an equilibrium much more stable than yesterday's, when with "conventional" weapons we could adjust losses and sacrifices to the advantages expected from a recourse to force.

It is not easy to explain that peace is all the more solid when, on either side, the weapons of retaliation are more numerous, feared, and in readiness. And also that the limitation of these weapons would be more dangerous than their proliferation. No one subscribes to such arguments willingly, though they unfortunately correspond to the realities of our age.

The campaign attempting to stop nuclear tests — in which the Japanese government has always participated vehemently — would be justified only if continuing the experimental explosions constituted a real danger for the future of humanity. As a matter of fact, it has not been proved that the risk is prohibitive, and it is certain that a number of high-altitude or underground experiments can be made without danger. But, in particular, if there is virtual unanimity as to the halting of these experiments, it is because everyone sees in their cessation the means of halting the dissemination of nuclear weapons, and believes in the final closing of that famous club henceforth limited to four members, thus bringing a solution to the problem of the nth Power. No more tests, no more new atomic countries. Politically, nothing could be more false.

If tomorrow, in fact, without ever having exploded a single nuclear charge, the Peking government were to offer Western and Soviet experts proofs of its nuclear experiments, and if it were to exhibit a certain number of explosive charges whose calculations and technology it justified, could the world still contest granting China the privileges it accords the other nuclear powers? Who could risk gambling on the nonfunctioning of weapons so skillfully studied and constructed? It is possible that they might not work; but what if they were to explode? What counts is that these explosive charges might exist and that the probability that they would work is high.

It would be wiser not to expect impossible results from the banning of the nuclear tests. Accession of new nations to the rank of atomic powers will not be impeded. It will be disadvantageous to the West to freeze the resources of nuclear armament at the present stage — that is, at the triumph of its offensive possibilities, the defensive domain having scarcely been touched.

When public opinion does not affect the government's conduct or, as is the case in the totalitarian countries, when public opinion is instructed to support the government's policy, it is of no importance that public opinion is ignorant of the rules of atomic strategy. On the other hand, the West has suffered greatly from the reactions — more emotional than rational — of a public opinion which it must nevertheless take into account. It is likely that the governments of the Western democracies will have no choice: either they must yield to public feeling, however ill founded, or else make a tremendous effort to educate that feeling. Of course the second alternative is the only possible one. It will ultimately appear ridiculous and even dangerous to devote billions to a policy of defense if, at the same time, important sums are not allotted to the explanation, justification, and popularization of that policy.

Some ten years ago, when the United States held the

monopoly of the atomic weapon, Western public opinion asked for no explanations. It was content with a dissymmetry of forces which seemed highly favorable to its own cause. This period is now past, particularly since the Kremlin has grasped the advantage to be derived from the obscurities and apparent paradoxes of the thermonuclear age. Consequently, to the difficult task of setting up a defensive system effective against a variety of threats, the West must also add another, without which, moreover, the first would become futile: obtaining the adherence and even the active support of public opinion.

Compared to the Western democracies, the authoritarian governments have the advantage of ignoring public opinion or, if necessary, of obliging it to support their policies. Since present-day international diplomacy is based on pressure or threats, it is natural that by gambling on the fear shown by Western public opinion or on its ignorance of the true laws of nuclear age diplomacy, the East should prove more successful.

Let us return to the definition of the strategy of dissuasion and the mathematical analogy we had adopted. The first of the two factors of the product:

$$\text{Value of the instruments of dissuasion} \times \text{Intention to use them should occasion arise}$$

can easily be positive. Western technology is equal to its imperatives. The present four nuclear powers will be joined by others. Merely by investing some hundreds of millions of dollars, industrialized nations like West Germany, Sweden, Italy, Switzerland, even Czechoslovakia and South Africa could afford the first weapons of a small atomic arsenal. This is true on either side of the iron curtain. But with one difference nevertheless: on the Western side, each nation is free to make the corresponding effort if it considers it possible and useful.

On the other hand, the second term of the product schematizing the policy of dissuasion is not necessarily positive. For a dozen years, facing a war of psychological attrition and Soviet encroachment, Western public opinion has most frequently ignored or opposed the interests of the free world. John Foster Dulles had the courage to struggle against this tendency and to pursue a policy to which only a few subscribed. Was the strategy of generalized dissuasion that of only one man? If it were not for the weight of public opinion, generalized dissuasion — that is, the policy of dissuasion applied to all conflict, whatever the stake or the means set in operation — would be effective. The corresponding techniques henceforth exist and most often all that is lacking is the courage to make use of them, or to appear to make use of them. In fact, since national unanimity could be achieved only in the face of a serious threat, the effectiveness of dissuasion is usually limited to the defense of the vital interests of the nation practicing this strategy. Between these nations there is a forced coexistence, and if further tension between them were to develop, it could be manifested only in a less direct, subtler manner than the old blackmail by war, ultimatum, or aggression. It is only if governments had complete freedom of action, or if they were assured of popular support, that they could effectively pursue the same policy of dissuasion for the defense of secondary goals. Consequently, even when they have the means to make use of it, the Western democracies are not at all comfortable in the corset of dissuasion. It is better suited to their respective sizes than to that of the world they mean to defend and develop.

IV   THE CONDITIONS OF SECURITY

Because it completely subverts every notion on which nations have always based their relationships, the nuclear
phenomenon remains incomprehensible. Humanity sees
in it only a scourge, projecting its memories of the great
wars of the past into an avalanche of atomic missiles and
contemplating a future of horrors. To humanity, it seems
absurd that the very omnipotence of these new weapons
can, at least temporarily, create a form of peace that
would be more stable — and more advantageous — than
any ever known. In the West, once one suggests the military and political use of the atom, one encounters contradictions and confusion.

We know that in 1954, once Lisbon and the subsequent
negotiations showed that the NATO nations could not
create an adequate defense system with merely conventional means, the interallied general staff was obliged to
offset its weakness in numbers by adding atomic weapons
to its panoply. Meeting in the Palais de Chaillot, the dele-
gations of the Atlantic nations approved the new concept

in December 1954. So that no one — particularly the Soviets — should be ignorant of this, Field Marshal Montgomery, then assistant to General Gruenther, Supreme
Allied Commander, discussed on several occasions and in
detail the laws of the new Atlantic strategy. Whatever the
form of an attack against any one of the NATO countries,
there would be a retaliation, and this retaliation would be
an atomic one. Either peace or nuclear war, Field Marshal
Montgomery proclaimed. Because of the disproportion
of mobilized and mobilizable masses on either side of the
iron curtain, Western Europe could not accept any other
alternative. Moreover, this one seemed reasonable to
everyone. Not only could the European governments, even
when aided by the United States, not afford the cost in men
and material resources of a conventional strategy, but
they even demanded the advantages of the new armament
techniques for themselves, since they had no desire to
provide troops for a defense system that could be made
impregnable by more modern means.

Three years later, when this bold conception had articulated a new military organization around the atomic
hypothesis, the same European nations began to protest:
"The forces of nuclear reprisal were overemphasized . . .
Infantry forces were being excessively reduced . . . The
risks taken were too great . . . Europe wanted to be defended, not atomized . . ." In short, the new arsenal had
been demanded in the name of economy and modernization; but no sooner was this arsenal constituted than it
was challenged.

The greater the effects of the powerful Soviet anti-
atomic campaign, the less the West can count on any fear
of its only weapons still capable of imposing the status.

quo. As the likelihood of an eventual recourse to the atom diminishes, the West should increase its conventional forces until they balance those on the other side of the iron curtain. It is part of the Russian strategy to confront the West with two impossibilities, that of the atom it is afraid to use, and that of the forces which it has neither the desire nor the means to muster. It is surprising that the Western statesmen, believing they are expressing the opinion of the people they govern, subscribe to atomic disarmament — on condition it is regularly checked, they specify in order to demonstrate a certain strictness — when it is the conventional forces which offer the double disadvantage of authorizing the recourse to force and, as far as the West is concerned, betraying her overwhelming material inferiority. Everyone behaves as if, on this side of the iron curtain, it were to the free world's interest to disarm until war is again likely and, in all probability, will be lost.

For the last fifteen years, there has been a great deal of discussion of atomic fission and its consequences, but the logic of the nuclear system remains esoteric. Ignorant of its laws, public opinion understands neither what it contributes nor what it costs.

Most of the measures the French government adopted with regard to NATO at the beginning of 1959 cannot be justified as defense or security moves, but only as considerations of foreign policy.

When, after having demanded ballistic missiles to modernize her contribution to collective defense system, France refused these weapons when the question arose of using them on her own territory, the "double check" formula was blamed. By "double check" is meant the two assents necessary to the use of these missiles: that of the nation on whose territory they are installed and that of the United States, the nation holding their atomic charges. Similar double-check formulas have been the object of agreements between Washington on the one hand and Rome and London on the other.

Of course, if a nation possesses the material means requisite to construct the instruments of dissuasion, and if it further publicizes its intention to use them if necessary, it thereby acquires the best possible assurance against subjugation. But it is obvious that not all nations can achieve this position, either materially or morally.

France, for instance, has just announced and proved that she could study and construct the forces necessary to the practice of "proportional dissuasion." If the efforts France is making give her such forces, she will simply have increased her security. If, on the other hand, technological development and world events reveal that France could not satisfy the justifiable ambitions she shows today, then she could still resort to the formula of the double check.

It has been said, and written, that the subjection of the double check limits the advantage these ballistic missiles could offer, and that in any case, it spoils whatever dissuasive value they might have on a national level. This criticism has no basis. It is clear that France — like any other nation, moreover — could not base its foreign policy on the threat of launching missiles with nuclear warheads. Occasionally dangerous, such an attitude would be completely ineffectual; it would not be taken seriously. It is hard to visualize Paris brandishing its atomic thunders against Moscow and gaining anything by it. One can imagine a nation threatening thermonuclear aggression only to discourage foreign intervention or to support another state of the NATO community. And whatever the adversary, this limitation exists: if powerful, the penalty would be enormous in relation to the stake defended; if weak, the whole world would oppose the practice of such blackmail. Hence thermonuclear missiles would be advantageous weapons for the French government only if quite exceptional circumstances made their use likely. In France's case the probability is still slight that the conditions of subjugation and total isolation should coincide, thereby justifying the political use of a national atomic arsenal. If, following a series of events difficult to anticipate today, this nation found itself in such an extremity, it would then be rational to expect one of the two checks to be lifted (the transfer agreement, for instance, might provide for a repeal of this check in cases of extreme danger) so that the weapon would assume the same dissuasive value as if it were wielded nationally. At the very least, the aggressor would have to take such an hypothesis into account. He would then be obliged to run as great a risk as if he were confronting a nation possessing its own ballistic and atomic arsenal. Although initially placed under a double check, in a crisis these missiles would have the virtues of the national weapons of dissuasion under normal circumstances. No doubt it is with this intention that Washington, since December 1957, has been pursuing a policy of "dissemination" of its atomic weapons. The MacMahon Law is tailored to the double check, and any potential aggressor must run the risk that America will lift hers. Even supposing that the collective guarantee did not function — out of pusillanimity, for instance — and that the United States could not directly intervene to the advantage of a threatened ally, a message would suffice to transform the instruments of a collective (or bilateral) "deterrent" into national weapons. We shall see below the advantages which the West as a whole could derive from the double-check formula. What is necessary is that the West keep up with the times and realize that the thermonuclear ballistic missiles have a political value only in extraordinary circumstances. Consequently missiles are not — as some still think — the modern version of yesterday's conventional weapons. No government can use them as it once used conventional weapons.

The Western governments still look back to the 1911 *coup d'Agadir,* when the Kaiser sent the *Panther* to the Moroccan port, proving to the world that Germany intended to defend her interests in Morocco or, at least, that the other powers would not have their hands free there. Wilhelm II made use of the resources of conventional armament, whose effects can be graduated. To put the *Panther* in Agadir's waters was to employ a scale of intervention ranging from waving the national flag to the landing of naval infantry units. Conventional weapons could be graduated in their use. The same is not the case with thermonuclear missiles. They cannot be used for similar "incidents" because their use would not be credible and because, consequently, not only would the threat be without effect but the nation making it would lose face. (Castro's government did not understand this when it declared that any American intervention in Cuba would release a rain of missiles on the United States. Nothing would happen, in all likelihood, and in any case certainly not a Soviet or thermonuclear reaction.) A missile is an all-or-nothing proposition. There is no nuance about its use, which determines an exact proportion between the risk taken and the value of the stake coveted. This is why the domain of the new weapons' political use is extremely limited.

If the use of the ballistico-nuclear arsenal is both so limited and so vital, it is easy to define the several danger criteria on which to base the bilateral agreements to be drawn up between the United States and each of its allies or groups of allies. It is enough to know that only a very small number of hostile manifestations can "deserve" a thermonuclear reaction.

No doubt, in the framework of a bilateral agreement between France and the United States, experts would decide that the fall of a nuclear missile on the soil of metropolitan France, the crossing of the Rhine in force by enemy divisions, the bombardment of the coast by an enemy fleet — in short, acts of aggression threatening the integrity of the national territory and the independence of the country — would constitute danger criteria whose verification would involve the lifting of the second "check," the missiles becoming "national" and the responsibility for their use reverting to France alone. The agreement would further specify that other cases of extreme peril were included which would also justify the lifting of the American check. This last clause would leave the two allies a certain margin of maneuver and would further widen the possible aggressor's zone of risk.

It may be objected that this formula alienates French sovereignty and that it makes the nation's security depend on the good will of an ally. This is not correct. Naturally

this thermonuclear arsenal could be used only in exceptional circumstances, as provided by the bilateral agreement. But is it conceivable that Paris should use it for
other purposes than those defined in common with Washington? There would be no fetters to the liberty of French
action, since the American constraint would only be manifested in circumstances which, in any case, would forbid
the use of these missiles. On the other hand, they would
play their role, since it would be understood that in case
of grave danger, the second check would be lifted and
these missiles would become the instruments of a strictly
national policy of dissuasion.

But if it is true that, even placed under a double check,
the arsenal of national dissuasion would fulfill its function without hampering the French government's freedom of action, what would be the consequent responsibility of the United States? Wouldn't Washington be made
responsible for a possible French reaction, and wouldn't
such a decentralization produce the same result as the
present centralization? Certainly not. It is to be expected
that before perpetrating his aggression or launching his
ultimatum the adversary might warn the United States
as follows: "If, according to the terms of the agreement
you have made with one of your allies, you transfer to its
government the control you exert over its missiles, you
will be responsible for what happens . . ." In the thermonuclear age, this accusation is meaningless, for it is not
possible to implement it, given the facts. If the American
reprisal forces are made invulnerable,[1] stigmatizing

---

[1] It is a matter of the now classic reasoning: if the American reprisal forces
are invulnerable, it is likely that the Soviet forces of aggression — or retaliation — are also invulnerable. In this case, urban centers constitute the

United States responsibility by attacking this nation would mean — for the U.S.S.R., for example — accepting its own destruction. It would be enough to answer the Soviet warning: "Responsible? Maybe! And afterwards?"

There would be no involvement of the guaranteeing power, at least no involvement that could be penalized. Vitally threatened, France would be free to choose — to use or renounce the threat of retaliation. However minimal, the risk of the national reaction would exist; hence dissuasion could be effective. As for the United States, as the guarantor nation it would merely have to reject an accusation and ignore a threat which, given the facts, could not be carried any further.

This solution has the advantage of granting a potential aggressor the initiative. On the other hand, in the framework of today's collective defense organization, it is the United States' responsibility to retaliate in nuclear terms against an attack launched by conventional forces against any of the NATO nations. And everyone knows what the consequences of such a reprisal would be. Nuclear decentralization and the generalization of the policy of national dissuasion would, on the contrary, force the aggressor to accept the responsibility and the risks inherent in any modification of the territorial status quo in Western Europe — and elsewhere, if such a policy were extended to other regions of the globe.

Lastly, the formula could reduce the proliferation of nuclear weapons. Each nation protests against these weap-

---

only possible targets. Consequently, using force would mean accepting mutual annihilation. This is why it is possible to reject the accusation and to consider the situation as a *fait accompli* against which the adversary could do nothing (save agree to mutual destruction).

ons and dreads the dangers with which they are supposed
to threaten humanity, but there is no example of a nation
which, possessing the financial and intellectual means,
has failed to devote them to becoming an atomic power.
The double-check system would no doubt forestall a
certain dissemination of effort with regard to nuclear re-
searches and achievements: their security assured, the nations would devote their resources to other more immediately rewarding activities. The transfer of missiles
placed under a double check would permit the gradual
modernization of this armament. Even if certain nations
succeeded, at the cost of great sacrifices, in constituting
an arsenal proper to dissuasion, they could scarcely keep
pace with the rest of the world's progress. Combined
with the leader-state, on the other hand, they would benefit from the results of its labors and would have some
opportunity of basing their security on weapons whose
quality was at least equivalent to that of their adversary's.

In June 1959, a dispatch from the Geneva Conference
announced that, according to a French spokesman, the sta-
tioning of Allied atomic forces on national territory would
be allowed only if France were consulted each time the
United States planned to use its nuclear force anywhere in
the world. Politically excellent, the argument was virtually worthless from a defense viewpoint. In recent years,
the accurate evaluation by both camps of the stake-risk
relation has dominated resistance to Communist expansionism. It was some time ago that Mr. Dulles formulated, with perhaps awkward frankness, the laws of safety
in the thermonuclear age and demonstrated the effectiveness of "brinkmanship." It is difficult to see how this pol-

icy — and there exists no alternative — would be taken
seriously if other nations than the one compelled to pursue it were associated with it, for it implies a determination before which the adversary retreats only because he
fears it to be unshakable. Would he have the same fear if
the assent of other governments (with necessarily disparate if not divergent interests) were substituted for this
single-power determination? What did the average
Frenchman say — and the average Englishman — when
Mr. Dulles took a stand on Quemoy, save to insist on discretion and hope for appeasement? How engage in the
diplomacy of local dissuasion if you are paralyzed by allies
insisting on being consulted in order to impose such paralysis all the more certainly? Would Peking and Moscow
have taken Mr. Dulles' warning seriously if they had
known him to be committed to London and Paris? De-
manding the extension of Allied responsibilities to the
whole of the anti-Soviet bloc was to be totally ignorant of
the laws of dissuasion. How could China believe that
France and Great Britain were ready to run the same risks
for Formosa as the United States? Would it ever be likely
that the European nations, absorbed by their own problems, more or less conscious of the imperatives of the
atomic age, would be prepared to pursue the apparently
dangerous strategy of dissuasion in the Far East? Moreover the question can be asked the other way around, as
well, the Suez incident providing the appropriate answer.

Certain Western European spokesmen have requested
the extension of the NATO guarantees to other geographic areas. As a matter of fact, it is the inverse movement that would be more rational. The greater the risk,
the more difficult it becomes to find partners capable of

uniting to take a stand: it is only natural that Norway should feel less vulnerable in Turkey than in Denmark. In a question of blackmail by thermonuclear assault, it is easier to resist regionally than at the level of an alliance grouping territories unequally threatened. By very reason of its success on the European continent, the NATO front has altered. But a defensive system adapted to the new threats could be made sounder by the addition of regional pacts — the American "commitment" giving each of these pacts their dissuasive power — than by the extension of the NATO treaty to other geographical areas. This concept should be at the origin of any adaptation of NATO to the new conditions. It is the proposal which will be made below.

Naturally a policy of local dissuasion is effective only if the potential aggressor knows that he will be threatening vital interests. This would be the case, since nothing is so vital to a people as its own existence as an independent and sovereign nation. The stake then "deserves" to be defended, even at the cost of enormous sacrifices. Blackmail by force would be dangerous to practice, for it must take into account what we have called the "national reflex." On the other hand, the greater the regions covered by a single collective guarantee, the less likely it is that there would be any resistance to pressure or the danger of a determined adversary.

Contrary to the orientation which the dangers of the last years of the pre-atomic age had given security conditions, it now seems that we must favor the geographical limitation of collective responsibilities rather than their generalization into larger groups. It is clear that the threat is world-wide, that it takes several forms and that it must be confronted in several ways, but everywhere with the same determination and according to the same general indications. However, if the threat should isolate its victim at one point of this enormous front, condemning him to choose between capitulation or destruction, it will appear obvious to many that the risks of solidarity have no relation to the limited stake to be defended.

Moreover, refusing bases to the American atomic pursuit bombers could impair not only the collective defense system but national interests as well, aside from the fact that the other allies assumed the risk inherent in the presence of these planes.

In this regard, the recent attitude of Great Britain furnishes an interesting example. After having abandoned mass production of the "Blue Streak" missile, London decided to improve the operational performance of its bombers by equipping them with air-to-surface missiles of the "Skybolt" type. Thus Great Britain hoped to reduce the vulnerability in flight of the V bombers which, though flying at high altitudes, were nonetheless relatively slow. The new equipment would enable them to launch a ballistic missile at a considerable distance from their targets and turn back without having to approach and penetrate heavily defended zones.

It remained to settle the problem posed by the vulnerability of the airfields, the classic weakness of the air-to-surface ballistic missile-bomber combination. Seeking invulnerability by field-to-field transfer is a good solution if the financial means are available, and particularly if the planes are authorized to land outside a relatively small national territory (as is particularly the case in Great Britain). After the incidents that followed the U-2 affair, reprisal planes, whether or not they carried explosive charges, have not been so politely received at foreign bases, even those located in friendly territory. Since the events that occurred in Japan during the difficult spring of 1960, the recommendations of the famous Nash report on the advantage of bases in foreign territory have been the object of new scrutiny. When questioned as to the orientation to be given to this study, Defense Secretary Thomas Gates replied that in examining the use of these bases it would be necessary to take into account the "political problems they created." Great Britain encounters similar difficulties in shifting its planes, and not every Commonwealth nation is prepared to receive them on its territory.

On the other hand, among the NATO nations, it is natural to proceed by reciprocity, Washington granting British planes rights analogous to those London accords to the Strategic Air Command planes. If the V bombers were able to change bases around the world by using the enormous network of air bases the Strategic Air Command still possesses, their erratic mobility would greatly contribute to their invulnerability and, assuring their "survival," would insure the significance of the British "deterrent." Tomorrow, the same problem of protection at bases will be posed for the bombers which figure in the "Law-French Program relative to certain military equipment" under the designation "system of strategic piloted weapons." The reciprocity of air-base privileges would have the double advantage of insuring the survival of the French strategic aircraft and also of confronting the possible aggressor with a dilemma: either destroy these planes wherever they may be — and consequently attack American territory as well — or risk "absorbing" the shock of a national reaction. Dispersing these planes throughout the NATO network would furnish the means of assuring their survival, the adversary being obliged to abandon force or attack the entire complex of NATO fields.

Moreover, similar agreements are necessary for missile-launching submarines. Although atomic propulsion gives them a great radius of action, the use of bases distributed around the world adds to their strategic effectiveness. Admiral H. O. Smith, commanding the American naval forces in Europe, announced at the end of June 1960, that Anglo-American negotiations concerning refueling of American Navy missile-launching submarines in certain British ports had been the object of important meetings. As the years pass and new techniques are developed, the interdependence of the Atlantic nations appears more and more essential. In this regard, let us recall that there is no contradiction between close association in order to create a defense system and the national feeling to increase the likelihood of use of an arsenal constituted by collective efforts. This is the solution to the present NATO crisis which will be offered below.

As for moral considerations, some say the judgment of the world will suffice to neutralize the advantage of force. They cannot envisage, for instance, the use of atomic blackmail. Human conscience would be outraged, and in a more heavily policed world it would no longer be possible to gamble on intimidation. There would be neither strong or weak powers, only mutual respect. To which it

is easy to reply that world-wide reprobation has not protected Hungary, and that the policy of nonresistance will
not produce, tomorrow, the results the Indian government anticipates. No examples exist to support the notion of mutual respect inspired by moral considerations.

Another solution to the problem of defense can be
provided by the stern determination to safeguard a certain way of life at any cost. The Western nations would
have to appear ready for the sacrifice. The thermonuclear armament has not condemned the effectiveness of
popular resistance to invasion and occupation, quite the
contrary. If, despite their social development, the nations
of Western Europe were still capable of assuming the attitude of the Spanish people to Napoleon's troops, they
would have a powerful safety potential, equivalent to the
most complete and the most diversified atomic stockpiles.
But the hypothesis is a gratuitous one. Experience — if
not logic — shows that there exists a certain relation between the virtues of guerrilla warriors and the standard of
living. The poorer a patrimony, the more fiercely it is defended. This law admits exceptions, but they do not
suffice to support a defensive system capable of impressing
a determined adversary. Nations like Switzerland or Sweden figure as exceptions, for their faculty of resistance to
aggression has not been put to the test for a long time.
But above all, despite their wealth, these two countries do
not represent — in the present instance — a stake of such
importance that major risks could be taken to violate their
neutrality. But their respective governments are no
longer content with their national reputations, and by
accumulating nuclear missiles seek to achieve the new
weapons of neutrality. By so doing, they may prefigure at
least a share of tomorrow's world, where the proliferation

of national stockpiles will not stand in the way of economic and ideological coalitions, but where, in security
matters, each nation will be neutral because it is capable
of making its neutrality respected, and is impotent to defend that of the others.

If moral suasion cannot outlaw the use of force, and if
disarmed neutrality has no chance of being respected, in
Europe at least, there remains the status quo — that is, a
system of collective defense based on an array of national
forces numerically modest yet significant enough to set
in motion the American atomic machinery.

Limited to the particular case of the defense of the
Western European territories covered by the Pact, this
concept would preserve its force for a long time to come
if entirely new strategic and political conditions had not
been created in the last three or four years.

All the criticisms of which NATO is now the object are
not without basis. This is because the Atlantic Alliance
was created under special circumstances: threatening a
Europe devoid of military power, the U.S.S.R. possessed
some 200 divisions, whereas the United States had a considerable head start in atomic weapons and its territory
was not vulnerable to the enormous power of the Soviet
conventional forces (which at the time could take only
Eurasia as their point of application). Subsequently, because of the Pact's very effectiveness, the threat has taken
other forms; because of the existence of weapons of massive destruction, armed struggle is outlawed, the atomic
bomb having banned war just as the machine gun had
proscribed close-order marches. Further, the American
territory can now be reached by the Soviet ballistic missiles and there is no longer an atomic dissymmetry.

Lastly, surrounded on all sides, the free world has grown

afraid. Giving vent to its anxiety and desperately looking for the key to the easy security it dreams of, it only adds to its weakness and its uncertainty. When Mr. Kennan wrote that the threat of massive retaliation had no real value because no one believed in it and because a system of collective security could not be based on weapons that could not be used, he was neglecting the enormous risk run by speculating on American passivity to a general attack with Europe as its stake. Naturally if the former American Ambassador to Moscow's words had been taken literally, the system would have collapsed. To doubt the effectiveness of the policy of atomic dissuasion pursued to the advantage of all nations by the United States releases a chain reaction with cumulative effects. Alarmed, the previously guaranteed nations seek other solutions, ranging from neutrality to national dissuasion. In every case, their attitude weakens the American determination to take for their sake the risks inherent in the policy of dissuasion.

But can it be otherwise? Must we not take into account a decisive evolution and, if there is still time, attempt to find a new defensive formula better adapted to present circumstances?

As far as the defense of Western Europe — and, in fact, of the free world — is concerned, most of the conditions prevailing at the moment of NATO's establishment have been completely transformed. It is easy to list these radical changes, and in the foregoing pages we have frequently alluded to the consequences of so swift a development. However, before proposing solutions adapted to the new conditions of strategy — and in order to justify their revolutionary character — it is necessary to review the factors that seem decisive enough to jeopardize a system which has proved its value over the last decade.

The Vulnerability of United States Territory

When the NATO treaty was signed, no one could foresee the advent of ballistic missiles and the vulnerability to their attack of the leader state that was at once bank, warehouse, and arsenal of the Western coalition.

The intercontinental ballistic missile with its thermonuclear warhead has deprived the United States of the advantage it derived from its geographical position with regard to Eurasia. Since the War of 1812 and the destruction of Washington by British troops, America has been able to intervene in the world's affairs without fearing the extension of any conflict to her own territory. Far from a Europe which had been the world's neuralgic zone for centuries, the United States had been privileged to play a decisive role there, merely by sending an expeditionary force to fight thousands of miles from her own national territory. Even during the Second World War, and despite the spectacular measures taken against the Japanese land and air threat, the American territory was never really in danger.

Henceforth America is as exposed as any nation of the Old World. The real strategic and political revolution is the new combination of the ballistic missile and the thermonuclear charge.

After 1954, of course, the West gradually realized that the Soviets were constituting a thermonuclear arsenal and acquiring the means to transport explosive charges by

mass-producing long-range bombers such as the turbine
"Bear" and also high-speed planes such as the quadrijet
"Bison." But at the time, one could still rely on the
distance to be covered and the effectiveness of a defensive
system opposing its short-range interceptor planes — light,
fast, and capable of close maneuvers — to heavy bombers
slowed still further by their enormous fuel loads. Up to
this time, though the Russians had constituted a stockpile
of thermonuclear charges and though the loss of the previous atomic monopoly was a reality, air defense was
still valid, and one could still speak of evolution rather
than of revolution.

But all strategic conditions were suddenly altered when
Mr. Khrushchev announced, at the end of August 1957,
that his technicians had launched ballistic missiles capable
of carrying thermonuclear charges.

To an already impressive arsenal, the Russians were
the first to add weapons that could not be countered. At
the time of the Soviet Premier's declaration, the anti-missile missile did not exist, and even today, the corresponding technology has advanced relatively little.

Further, the several hours' alert the United States
counted on in case of attack was reduced to some tens of
minutes. By their speed and their range, the ballistic
missiles shrank space and virtually annihilated the advantages the Strategic Air Command and the Continental Defense Command could derive from the warning
provided by the distribution of American bases around
the periphery of the communist world. Even by creating
new means of long-range detection and by using reconnaissance satellites, no more than twenty to thirty minutes' alert could henceforth be counted on.

The Soviets had just given the world proofs of a splendid scientific achievement. It was apparent that they owed it to none but their own efforts. It was no longer possible to invoke espionage or the utilization of another nation's secrets, as had been the case at the time of the first Soviet atomic explosion. Naturally there existed the German precedent of the V-2's, but that was a remote one and its techniques were obviously outdated. The Russian successes struck a blow at the liberal dogma the West had complacently paraded as the only possible system capable of satisfying the requirements of scientific development. The American head start in research was contested, and the Western monopoly of technological progress was now to be shared with a regime which had been dismissed as incapable of stimulating scientific thought and exploiting its manifestations. The world — or that part of it which was uncommitted — admired an achievement which it attributed less to the wealth than to the virtues of an effective system, based on intelligent and rigorous planning.

The equilibrium between the two atomic forces of dissuasion, American and Soviet, had been destroyed. The Strategic Air Command bombers would be vulnerable at their airfields, even when these fields were located several thousand kilometers from Soviet territory, whereas the location of the Russian launching sites — which, moreover, were harder to destroy than these fields — was not generally known. From a situation of superiority, the United States moved to a state of inferiority, at least according to the strict logic of warfare. If the United States should ever wield the threat of retaliation, Moscow would know that such a reprisal was more likely to aim at the

Soviet urban centers than the Soviet air bases and, more generally, the Soviet armed forces. The same reasoning deprives America of her old faculty of attacking first. Preventive warfare, occasionally referred to in America, can no longer achieve its purpose, for to destroy the Soviet cities without having first — or at least simultaneously — neutralized the Russian means of reprisal means to provoke retaliation and, consequently, to culminate in mutual annihilation. If, for instance, the U.S.S.R. openly attacked the Western European states now protected by NATO — in other words, by American military power — and if this attack were conducted with conventionally armed forces, the Soviets would put the United States in a difficult situation because intercontinental ballistic missiles figure in both opposing arsenals. As we have said, Washington's alternative would be as follows: either retaliate against the Soviet habitat — the only static, known, and easily reached target — in which case, there would be reprisals and American cities would also be destroyed; or else attempt a counterbattery — that is, the annihilation of the Soviet launching sites, but in this case an enormous numerical superiority would be necessary, of which it is highly unlikely that Moscow would ever leave the advantage to Washington. It is even probable that either side would have to give up constituting a force of ballistic missiles numerically large enough to permit a counterbattery strategy.

Calculations show — and the corresponding figures have been given above — that anti-launching-site forces must be numerically stronger than those they intend to destroy. When both sides abandon concrete and underground storage for semipermanent mobility of their missiles, this anti-site potential becomes — theoretically, at least — infinitely large. Consequently, Washington, like Moscow, would probably have to abandon acquiring a counterbattery arsenal. When this is the case, the United States and the U.S.S.R. would be able to use their nuclear stockpiles only at the risk of mutual annihilation. Atomic aggression would no longer be able to paralyze reprisal. And striking first could lead to being destroyed second. Striking second, in retaliation for either a conventional or an atomic attack, would entail annihilation by vengeance. Valid for one side as for the other and known to each, the logic of these exchanges must create, between the two major thermonuclear powers — and between them only — a singularly stable balance, much more stable than if atomic weapons did not exist or than if the stockpiles had been destroyed, reverting to the past's uncertainties and to the old estimate of the relation of conventional forces. On the other hand, the security of the nations now guaranteed by a possible nuclear intervention becomes more precarious.

Between the political conditions that existed some dozen years ago and those now apparent, there are virtually no points in common. When, after the end of the Second World War, in 1945 and 1947, the aggressive intentions of the communist bloc became evident, the United States was able to shift in a few years from a policy of noncommitment to the establishment of a huge collective system embracing almost all of the noncommunist nations. The latter, guaranteed by a powerful and invulnerable nation, readily accepted the few inconveniences of such a form of security. As for the United States, it could readily run the risks inherent in this policy of

general commitment. It has been said that if the Second
World War had cost humanity over fifty million lives, the
United States, by the quality of its technology, the force of
its organization, but especially because of its privileged
geographical position, had played the leading role while
losing less than one per cent of the total number of victims. This century-old invulnerability no longer exists.
By adding the intercontinental ballistic missile to its panoply, the U.S.S.R. has destroyed — no doubt for good —
the *données* of American "geo-strategy." The long-range
ballistic missile invalidates — at least in part — the advantages which America and her allies derived from the
collective system they had just established. It is essential
that Washington realize that future commitment for the
sake of other nations presents considerable risks. As for
the allies, aware of the dangers which America would
have to accept in protecting them, they are beginning to
question the solidity of a guarantee which has become the
source of dangers much more critical than they were yesterday. Of course, if Western public opinion on both
sides of the Atlantic were better informed of the laws of
nuclear strategy, and if the policy of dissuasion had not
kept its esoteric character, the intercontinental ballistic
missile would not have had such psychological and political impact. In practical terms, this temporary Soviet advantage does not completely alter the balance of forces,
and the American policy of dissuasion retains at least a
large share of its power. But the dominant fact is that the
American people must gradually realize that they too, are
now in the front line. And though they are vulnerable to
an adversary's attacks, they remain geographically as remote from their allies as before. The evolution of the
technology of weapons seems to proceed against the in-

terests of the free world. It serves the aggressor, who is henceforth capable of delivering a deadly blow to the United States, without thereby consolidating allies whose security does not depend only on the Strategic Air Command's ballistic missiles, but on the presence of American soldiers on their territory.

And how believe that the Strategic Air Command would use its weapons of massive destruction for the sake of a third party, if America thereby risked, in reprisal, a setback of two centuries from the extent of the damages suffered!

Then what becomes of the indispensable credibility of the reprisal against aggression? Of course, this is only one panel of the diptych of dissuasion. The aggressor must also run this risk before imposing his estimate upon his future victim. But since American impunity is no longer assured and since Western public opinion — like many Western governments — does not understand the subtleties of an entirely new strategic situation, the question arises of discovering the present validity of a defense system based not only on the invulnerability of the guaranteeing power, but on the latter's capacity to launch attacks without being obliged to "receive" them.

These discoveries and prospects are at the origin of the present difficulties NATO is encountering. The governments which imagine they possess the necessary resources are trying to add to those of collective dissuasion the means of a national policy of dissuasion. They are thereby attempting to insure themselves against the possible collapse of a system that in their eyes has become highly uncertain.

There remains one means of escaping the dilemma in which Washington would be placed if Western Europe

were threatened with invasion by Soviet land divisions
without atomic armament but numerically vastly superior: to deploy, as close as possible to the iron curtain,
American and European forces so numerous — or so powerful — that the westward march of the Russian "conventional" divisions would appear extremely costly to the assailant. The greater the disproportion of conventional
means, the sooner the Western forces would resort to their
low- and medium-power atomic arsenal. These explosives
re-establish the equilibrium in so far as they cancel out
the virtues of the heavy battalions and start up the "escalator" mechanism and consequently lead to the abandonment of force.

It is not a matter of waging limited atomic war, but —
since it would be likely that the weaker power would resort to it — the aggressor must anticipate the "rise" in the
scale of destructive power and weigh the risks before taking action. Of course, he knows that an atomic skirmish
would lead to a kind of mutual suicide, but he is also
aware that he would have nothing to gain from an exchange of atomic attacks delivered on either side of the
iron curtain. For the aggressor does not know how far
such a confrontation would go. It is quite likely that it
would go far, and that the extent of the damages suffered
would soon exceed the value of the stake desired, in this
case Western Europe itself.

The formula has its dangers. Since its use is imposed by
the inequality of the forces confronting each other, the
nuclear explosive obviously determines a new structure
of the armed forces, and this adaptation to the conditions
of the "minor atomic war" is, in fact, irreversible. Because the power of destruction by unit-of-fire would then

be considerably increased, the number of combatants could be reduced.[1] Nevertheless, these forces would be ineffectual when confronting conventionally armed forces that were numerically stronger. Because in a nuclear war, the essential performance required of armament matériel is the "survival" of massive destruction, such matériel would be penalized if it had to be used in a conventional war.

For example, planes that are still being built for combat must be able to escape the atomic explosion by mobility and dispersion. In order to do so, they will need to use take-off and landing platforms of small dimensions. This necessity limits their performance in other areas. During a conflict in which tactical atomic weapons would not be used, these planes would no doubt be inferior to conventional matériel.

But what other solution is there? Can the West achieve equilibrium with the East in some other way? Is it even imaginable that it should accumulate manpower in order to reach numerical parity? Can it deny what it is trying to defend and ignore an intellectual and social revolution that forbids recourse to heavy battalions? How stupid would be a policy which ignores the very characteristics of Western civilization and which, renouncing the super-technique that imposes the renunciation of force, opposes division to division and the Western air and naval squadrons to Eastern, thereby creating the conditions of war and most likely of the most dreadful defeat.

The effectiveness of the Allied atomic and conventional

1 Expert opinions differ. The Russians calculate that their forces should be increased, because of their losses. But will the combatant agree to continue the struggle while supporting losses so exorbitant?

system "engaged" in Europe is demonstrated by the furious remarks Mr. Khrushchev continues to make about it. All levels of Soviet policy seek primarily the neutralization of the contact zone, the creation of a "denuclearized" strip of territory and, directly or indirectly, the withdrawal of the American forces which possess atomic armament of small and medium caliber and which alone are able to confront the aggressor, in his turn, with a dilemma: either negotiation before going too far on the "escalator" or the exchange of thermonuclear attacks. If the real consequences of the policy of "disengagement" were better known, it would lose its attractions. "Disengagement" would in fact make it materially impossible for the United States to extend its guarantee.

Europe would be alone. Of course, there would be no conflict; the disproportion of means is, in fact, obvious enough for resistance to appear futile to everyone. Not force, but merely its shadow would be the decisive factor.

If, then, cowardice or naïveté were to triumph, and if, impelled by fear or excessive complacency, the Western defense structure were to crumble, would it be necessary to shift from an Atlantic to a European focus? If this European community really existed and if it had succeeded, by consolidating its intellectual and material resources, in creating an atomic arsenal, would it be in a better position to resist the pressures of war than the Atlantic world had been? Or rather, if out of ignorance or cowardice, the West itself condemned the Atlantic defense system to failure, would the nations of Western Europe find a substitute in their union? Close to the sources of danger, would the European nations agree to run a collective risk analogous to that which the United

States runs in guaranteeing a large portion of the free world?

If these European nations were collectively and directly threatened, the answer would perhaps be affirmative. But would there be the same unanimity if it were a question of defending only one of these European nations? Would this kind of collective dissuasion maintain the slightest value when transferred by several governments to territories unequally exposed? Would it even appear likely that there would be some agreement over the use of the weapons of dissuasion for the sake of one of the member nations of the European community? Reassured by the aggressor, would the others not abandon a carefully isolated victim? For the concept of dissuasion to have any validity, Europe must be "a political whole, a fatherland." And more. Even united, Europe would not have the means to implement a counterbattery or anti-launching-site strategy. The use of its forces, collectively mustered and united into an army, would naturally lead to reprisals and, consequently, to a kind of self-destruction. The prospect is the same for any nation pursuing the policy of dissuasion with thermonuclear weapons. But, already difficult for one nation to accept when its own existence is at stake, dissuasion would be far more so for a *group* of nations. Such a group would have to accept collective annihilation rather than the abandonment of any constituent member that was under attack.

In the eyes of the potential aggressor, would it be more likely that Western Europe, rather than America, would take this risk? Would he be more impressed by the apparent union of five or six European nations than by the United States of America alone? It is obvious that a dissuasion force provided by the governments of Paris, London, Bonn, Rome, Brussels, and The Hague, aside from being limited in importance and in quality, would frighten no one. Who would even suppose there could be any unanimity as to its conditions of possible use? In the framework of the studies undertaken by the Council on Foreign Relations in New York, Ben Moore has published a book[1] in which, arguing from the close interdependence of the European nations, he asks for the establishment of a European "deterrent." The identity of interests which binds the free nations of the Old World together no longer exists between Europe and America, Mr. Moore declares. "The Americans fear that the Europeans may be opposed to a Western retaliation launched from European soil against a Soviet attack, or else the Europeans fear that the American hesitations will compromise the effectiveness of the 'deterrent.'"

Perhaps the bonds of the Atlantic world *have* grown weaker, but Mr. Moore attributes to the community of interests of the European nations a power which it is unfortunately far from having.

The structure of atomic defense that would be based on the present territorial mosaic, aside from breaking up the Atlantic world and further separating Europe from America, would be chiefly hampered by the fact that it is likely to collapse at the first test. Depending on consultations among governments, it would be less solid than the purely national American deterrent. It would weaken the Alliance without reinforcing the defense of the Western European nations.

The notion has recently been discussed in Great Britain

[1] *NATO and the Future of Europe.*

and also in the Western Union Organization by a British member of Parliament, Mr. Mulley. In political terms, his proposition was attractive. It would contribute to the construction of a united Europe, which each nation must desire. But it had the disadvantage of being senseless in military terms. Had its promoters been able to free themselves from the weight of history, had they realized the significance to a nation of the risks of nuclear conflict, it would probably never have been formulated.

Still another formula: instead of depending on the Strategic Air Command, the instruments of dissuasion could be mustered under the authority of a NATO command. Consequently the Atlantic nations could feel that their protection did not derive from an American decision alone. They would at least discuss the conditions under which retaliation would be launched. But, in the case in point, it is less the opinion of the guaranteed nation than that of the potential aggressor which counts. If the latter knew that the functioning of the reprisal forces was subordinate to the agreement of some fifteen governments, he would have much less to fear from these forces than from those the American government possessed in its own right, even when acting for the sake of other nations. To this formula one can make the same objection, that its only difference from the European deterrent is that the American contribution would no doubt permit the NATO instruments of dissuasion to be more powerful — if not more effective — than those of a Europe consisting of associated nations confronting the danger and probably divided once it was manifest.

The foregoing analysis leads to the national deterrent. Not that it is easy to establish or that it is all-powerful.

But it is logical that the nation possessing weapons of dissuasion should take the risk of using them when its very
existence is threatened. Nationally wielded, the deterrent
imposes at least a certain credibility and a certain fear. It
presents the advantage of having a meaning only in the
one circumstance in which it can be used: the threat of
subjugation, blackmail by thermonuclear annihilation,
etc. To be effective, it need only represent a quantity of
destruction equivalent to the advantages the aggressor
would derive from the "absorption" of the nation it
threatens.[1] In other words, the national means of dissuasion can be limited; and, in any case, can be less important, less powerful than those indispensable to the safety
of a large territorial unit.

Another argument in favor of the national deterrent, if
one takes into account the probable development of armament techniques, is that no nation, whatever its power,
could pursue an anti-launching-site strategy against the
Soviets. Each would have to enforce dissuasion by threatening to annihilate the adversary's urban potential, and
this is as true of the United States — and also of the
U.S.S.R. — as of the nth Power to possess an atomic arsenal. Naturally this equality of the Great, Middle, and
Small Powers before the law of missiles exists only if the
numerical weakness of certain forces does not condemn
them to destruction. Nations like the United States and
the U.S.S.R. would have the means of an anti-launching-
site strategy if they dealt with nations much less richly
provided than themselves and if these nations did not
protect their missiles by mobility or burial underground.

[1] General P. Stehlin, "Adaptation of the Instrument of Defense to the
Technological Revolution." *Revue Militaire Générale,* February 1959.

But confronting Soviet (or American) power, all nations are in the same class. Whether they possess, tomorrow, a thousand Atlas, Titan, or Minuteman missiles, like the United States, or fifty Thor missiles like Great Britain, they could base their security only on an anti-city strategy. In other words, faced with an alternative of servitude or invasion, a nation could gamble on the policy of dissuasion to save its independence. But it would have to run the risk of being annihilated, for if it failed the policy of dissuasion would lead to total destruction. And this is as true for the Great Powers among themselves as for the Small and Medium Powers in relation to the Great Powers.

But to choose dissuasion is not as aberrant as it seems, since at worst — the destruction being mutual though unequal — the potential aggressor would be obliged to renounce provoking a trial by force. Of course the validity of such a policy can be questioned. That is why it has meaning only if it is pursued to the exclusive advantage of the nation adopting it. If the determination to resist can lead a nation to suicide, it is because it is of national inspiration.

National dissuasion offers the Western nations one further advantage which is not yet measured at its worth. It authorizes the creation of a defense instrument which need not depend on popular consent and which can therefore be more influential than a classical system based on the adherence and support of the masses. Yesterday there was no such thing as a defense organization which did not consist of the nation as a whole. The governing body accepted a certain military system, voted the corresponding budget, established the length of military service; the nation furnished the men and influenced its government's defense policy. As long as an armed force was based on the mustering of as great a number of men as possible, this was the case. The new weapons have changed everything. A kind of Pretorian Guard — but a guard under the government's orders — is enough to set in action an enormous power of destruction, and consequently to materialize a respectable dissuasion force. Popular adherence is no longer indispensable to the use of this force, since it need number only a relatively few men. The potential aggressor can no longer gamble on the power of his victim's public opinion, since it exerts no control over this reprisal force. Consequently such an instrument of defense is more to be feared than the old one. In the case of a conflict between the present conventional forces of the Western European nations and those of Eastern Europe, all Western resistance would appear doomed to failure and the sacrifice would seem futile to everyone. On the contrary the nuclear weapon, wielded by a small body of men, ignores the inequality of forces, the subjectivity of public opinion, the paralysis of great numbers. It alone can guarantee the weak against the appetites of the strong.

But though the policy of a national deterrent has at least the advantage of making the adversary reflect before attacking, if widely practiced it would lead to a kind of juxtaposition of states, friendly in all matters but neutral toward each other with regard to security, each defending its patrimony but none ready to risk helping the next, even if the latter were next door.

Each nation being impregnable, in theory at least, a form of the status quo would be created which would appear all the firmer for depending on a unanimously dreaded threat. But in practical terms, such stability would not necessarily exist. By reason of the subjective nature of dissuasion — even when it is not pursued by a power for the sake of its allies, but on the national level — equilibrium would be firm here and precarious there. In some hands the arsenal of dissuasion would not be dreaded, whereas wielded by others it would have an enormous power of intimidation.

In Western Europe, the collective defense system would be put to the test, each member nation of NATO supposing it could defend itself and regarding the Alliance as nothing but a source of dangerous obligations. If the national deterrents really insured the security of each, and consequently of all, the difficulty would not be great and, like the other alliances, the Pact would have served its purpose. But the reality is quite different: Only two nations actually possess an atomic panoply; the dissemination of American ballistic missiles gives certain guarantees to the nations which have agreed to install them on their territory; lastly, for most Western European nations the establishment of national dissuasion forces — even in proportion to the stake these nations represent collectively — is subordinated to political, financial, and technological considerations. It will take years for the concept of a common defense to be replaced by that of a front held by the array of national forces of dissuasion. An intermediary formula must therefore be devised.

These are the multiple consequences of the swift development of the techniques of offensive armament we have been witnessing lately. But since NATO's establishment, other modifications, almost as important, have contributed to revolutionizing the conditions of world strategy.

The Cost of Modern Weapons

It is a truism to speak of the cost of modern weapons. Everyone knows the amounts that must be spent on the planning of a bomber or the construction of a missile-launching submarine. Asking an American Senate budget committee to authorize the purchase of new planes for the Navy, Admiral R. E. Dixon, head of the Bureau of Naval Aeronautics, announced that each F8U-3 heavy fighter plane cost about ten million dollars. As for the B-52 bomber, already manufactured by the hundreds, it was then being sold to the American air force (with the necessary spare parts) for eight million dollars. The B-70 Valkyrie bomber, which was to replace the B-52, would cost at least three times as much.[1] The manufacturer already estimated that its planning would require at least seventy times the amount of man hours required for the planning of the Boeing B-17 which constituted the American bomber force during the Second World War. When the 60,000-ton aircraft carrier *Independence* was launched, the Navy announced that its cost was two hundred million dollars. In his State of the Union message of January 1959, President Eisenhower set at thirty-five million dollars the cost of a single Atlas ballistic missile placed in firing position, and at fifty million dollars the cost of one of the atomic submarines now being mass-produced.

But what is significant today is less the constant increase of the cost of combat matériel than the obligation to widen its scale. Place has had to be made alongside con-

[1] Recently the mass-production cost of the B-70 was estimated at over forty-five million dollars.

ventional matériel for the new explosives, then for missiles, and finally for space techniques. Reconnaissance, detection, communication, and navigation satellites are appearing in the military panoply, one after another. The United States Defense Department is obliged to spend almost four million dollars a year for planning and research alone. And still the whole extent of areas to be explored has not been covered. In 1960 the British allotted about 650 million pounds sterling to the whole of their research, planning, and armament manufacture program. It is obvious that they cannot follow the lead the two Great Powers have set.

The almost frenzied increase of the unit prices of armament matériel and the necessity of possessing weapons of an increasingly wide scale are not the only factors. The rate at which the armament techniques develop must also be considered. In this regard, the Blue Streak incident is significant. At the time the British created this missile, it was to be expected that survival in terms of burial underground, protection by concrete, or mobility would be neglected: the only factor relied on was the greatly reduced dimensions of the launching platform. It was believed, at the time, that ballistic missiles would be relatively imprecise and their average firing error was equivalent to .3 or .4 per cent of their range. Calculation then showed that in order to destroy a Blue Streak on its platform with an adequate probability of success — say 90 per cent — it would be necessary to launch against it some twenty or thirty missiles fitted with one-megaton warheads. The enemy potentialities were thus easily saturated and dissuasion therefore performed its work. But the guiding of missiles has subsequently advanced, radio-inertia has become a factor, the inertia platforms are improved daily, and exactitudes ten to twenty times greater than what was anticipated only four or five years ago have been achieved.[1] It was no longer thirty missiles which were necessary, but less than three. It was therefore necessary to abandon the manufacture of the Blue Streak and to adopt a new concept. London decided to improve its fleet of subsonic bombers by furnishing them with the air-to-surface Skybolt missile which the United States Air Force planned to manufacture for its B-52's. And at the same time it is likely that, renouncing a new attempt analogous to that of the Blue Streak, London will base its dissuasion policy on the Thor missiles received from the United States and will in the future negotiate the transfer of some Polaris or other missiles already manufactured and tested by Washington.

These figures and this example show that in the realm of armaments, too, the situation is now different from what it was at the time of the signing of the NATO Pact.

Gaps between the member states were much narrower than they are today. Of course, the array of European national contributions was already inadequate to defend Western Europe effectively, and the enormous American "balance" was decisive. In financial and military terms, it was this American contribution which constituted the principal. But it was above all the planes and heavy ships and the nuclear explosive that represented the leader state's particular contribution. For the rest, and thanks to American economic aid, Europe managed to cut a respectable figure.

[1] During one of the launching tests against a target located in the Pacific, a Soviet missile traveled 7767 miles and would have reached a point situated 1.24 miles from the target. This extremely slight error is less than .02 per cent of the range.

Today, the European members of NATO have remained virtually where they were ten years ago. The cost of a complete modern arsenal has increased much faster than their individual gross national product (although their economic situation is flourishing). At the same time, the United States and Russia have devoted enormous sums to exploration of the new technological areas, to diversification of the atomic weapon, to missile carriers, to new means of propulsion, to space itself.

Taken separately, the most powerful nations of Europe cannot maintain their conventional forces and at the same time approach the domain of the heavy missile, of long-range detection, of warning and reconnaissance satellites, of nuclear explosives of varying power. Whether it is the new sources of propulsive energy, the new explosives or the new carrying vehicles that are at stake, the two Great Powers have a permanent head start. In the hierarchy of power, Europe is sliding downward, daily increasing its distance from the U.S.A. and the U.S.S.R.; tomorrow it will be far behind still other nations beginning their ascent only today. Like Islam, which until the seventeenth century manufactured weapons similar to those of the other European powers but which, at the dawn of the industrial age, was no longer capable of following France and Great Britain and of entering the age of artillery, the nations of Western Europe now stand at the crossroads: either they accept their backwardness and admit their future dependence, or else they agree to join forces in order to shift from a too-narrow national level to the European or rather to the Atlantic level, which is more on the scale of the task to be accomplished.

In 1954, conscious of the price of a nationalism already

outdated by financial, technological, and military requirements, General Norstad, then Air Deputy to General Gruenther, the Supreme Allied Commander, had drawn up the balance sheet of the situation in the domain of air forces alone. According to his study, it appeared that the 5000 warplanes then in service in Western Europe were of more than twenty-five different types. And, in fact, the diversity of this matériel was even greater, since one model, the F-84, comprised nearly 50 per cent of the American planes then existing. In other words, the Allied air forces deployed in Western Europe included some 2500 combat planes of twenty-four different models. In the realm of aircraft for training, the diversity was greater still. One can imagine the cost of such diversity, both in terms of planning and of mass production. And it is easy to understand the complexity of the corresponding technical supply services.

Yet the planning and production of armament remained a national privilege, and each nation followed a path which has now become an impasse for most of them. This fact is more apparent today than during the Treaty's first years, and the Blue Streak incident has just made it brutally obvious to the British. It is clear, moreover, that the nature of scientific progress is henceforth so unforeseeable that several paths must be explored at once without expecting to find results at the end of each.[1] Not only is each research and development scheme costlier, but it is necessary to undertake a great number of them to have any chances of keeping up with the rate of scientific discovery.

Consequently we have a situation different from the one that existed a dozen years ago.

[1] Burton Klein, *Fortune*, May 1958.

The Technological Race

"As the art of war grows more complicated, technology becomes more and more important. As a matter of fact, if the strategy of the West — or of the Soviets — were to triumph without resorting to force, it is in the domain of technology that the decision would occur, for technology — with the exception of war itself — contains all the elements of the decision," wrote General Gavin in his *War and Peace in the Space Age*. In military terms, no one contests the value of scientific and technological progress. The laws of the new strategy, the character of the policy of dissuasion, the weight of public opinion have all shown the power and effectiveness of demonstrations as spectacular as the launching of the first Soviet satellites. The credibility of an American reprisal against a possible Soviet threat diminished once it became obvious that the Soviets possessed a powerful ballistic arsenal. The man in the street believes that if there had been no Sputniks, Mr. Khrushchev would never have made his trip to the United States.

Although in military terms a certain technological advance is no longer so decisive as it might have been some fifteen years ago, public opinion is still as sensitive to it. The U.S.S.R. has been able to shift the struggle to this terrain, and the West cannot afford to lag behind. If it is satisfied to remain in second place, it will lose both the means of insuring its defense and furnish proof of the inferiority of the political and social system it prides itself on.

It is for this reason, for instance, that the West cannot lose the scientific and technological race and still nurse the chimerical hope of insuring its security with conventional forces. Such a concept fails to hold water even if the West possessed a head start and managed to increase it. But if the U.S.S.R. were to emerge victorious, it would be obvious that superiority of technology would be joined to that of numbers, and consequently that the issue of the conflict would not be in doubt.

It is incumbent upon the United States to enter this technological race and to win it. It is likely, moreover, that in such a competition, the European contribution would be useful, perhaps even decisive.

Here again, the Atlantic world is faced with the same alternative: either it remains divided, the struggle is harder, even condemned to failure, and the European nations are alienated; or else resources are shared, all participate in the ordeal, each rising in the hierarchy of knowledge and power, and the chances of emerging victorious are larger.

There was no question, ten years ago, of participating so fiercely in such a competition. The Atlantic world must now divert from the resources devoted to its defense the means of emerging victorious in the technological race as well.

The Underdeveloped Nations

Another relatively new problem is that of the so-called underdeveloped nations. Ten years ago, the question might have arisen how the richest nations were to go

about improving material conditions of existence throughout the world. But the Soviet threat appeared both urgent and decisive enough for the West to deal with it by
creating a military instrument primarily intended to protect the territory of Western Europe from invasion. The
underdeveloped nations were not yet the springboards of
the gradual encirclement of the great Western Powers.
No one suggested a relation between the defense of Western Europe and aid to the underdeveloped nations.

In recent years, the scales have fallen from our eyes.
We have begun to realize that 70 per cent of the world's
inhabitants have an average annual income of less than
three hundred dollars, whereas in the United States the
corresponding figure is some 2600 dollars. And 50 per
cent of the human beings on earth must content themselves with an average of less than the equivalent of one
hundred dollars a year — in other words, between twenty-
five and thirty times less than the theoretical income of
the American citizen. The economists, moreover, make
no secret of the fact that the gap is widening, the rich
growing richer faster than the poorest can improve their
lot.

It follows that the remedy must be planned and administrated without alluding to the vicissitudes of the
cold war. When the Marshall Plan was being prepared, its
editors defined its goals in these terms: "Our undertak-
ing is not directed against any nation or doctrine, but
against hunger, poverty, despair and chaos. We are trying to revive throughout the world an economy healthy
enough so that the social and political conditions can develop under which free institutions may exist . . ."

If an enormous plan of aid must be undertaken, it is by

the mediation of an interallied organization and with the purpose of developing to their advantage the resources of the nations thus aided. But whatever the formula adopted, it will be essential that, in so far as it concerns them, the member nations of the Alliance produce from their own resources the subsidies they will devote to this form of collective assistance. Having paid the price of the new weapons, having confronted the problems posed by the diversification of armament techniques, having entered, at the cost of millions, the technological race, they must also find additional means to combat "hunger and chaos" for the sake of almost a billion human beings.

The Improvement of the Standard of Living of the Solvent Nations

The underdeveloped nations are not the only ones to claim the assistance which would allow them to move ahead. The nations richly provided for are also trying to improve their living conditions without endangering their security. As the nations of Western Europe d their economies, they are reducing the percentage of subsidies allocated to their defense. Most European nations would prefer either to cancel obligatory military service or to reduce its length. The advocates of a defense policy based solely on conventional forces would do well to take this tendency into account. It is not enough to inventory the respective human resources of the NATO nations and those of the Warsaw Pact. In the nuclear age, such a comparison is senseless.

The economic and social development of the Western

nations scarcely predisposes them to deliberate sacrifice. To be willing to oppose division to division, they would have to feel that their sacrifice was not in vain, that they could be certain of emerging victorious, and also that the struggle would be pursued with equal weapons. Who today believes such conditions could be realized in Europe?

Eminent specialists recently proposed a solution to the problem of conventional armed forces: ". . . An important and effective reserve army is the key to any strategy capable of satisfying either the needs of a world war, of a limited conflict or of a paramilitary confrontation . . ." wrote Mr. Frederick M. Stern in *Orbis* (Winter 1960). And Mr. Stern continued: ". . . There exists a military organization which would permit the free nations to fill the gaps which exist in their defense system and, forming the complement of the forces already created, to confront the present conflict in all its aspects . . . This organization is that of the army of citizens." And the author quotes as an example forces of the Swiss, Israeli, or Australian types. In Switzerland, Mr. Urs Schwarz[1] advanced a similar notion and suggested the reinforcement of NATO with the aid of militia forces.

The proposal is attractive. But it is not realistic, for it is based on a false premise. The two authors suppose, in fact, that the use — even widespread — of weapons of massive destruction will not undermine the belligerents' determination to fight. How can we follow Mr. Schwarz, who also transposes to the atomic age the militia systems that have worked wonders in Australia, New Zealand, Canada, Israel, or Switzerland, when such organizations have shown their worth only in peacetime or against ad-

[1] *Neue Zürcher Zeitung*, February 21, 1960.

versaries not possessing the new weapons? Confronting
the military threat which the U.S.S.R. represents today
(and which China will materialize tomorrow), what is to
prevent the Western militiaman from reasoning as follows: "If the U.S.S.R. resorts to force, it is because she believes she will emerge victorious in military terms; now,
since this nation possesses both numerical superiority and
the complete panoply of conventional and atomic weapons, it is natural that it should use these weapons, up to
and including the most powerful ones, rather than lose;
what is the use, under these conditions, of proceeding to
extremes of sacrifice since, in any case, the assailant is in
a position to triumph by using an explosive of massive destruction against which man is defenseless?" Do Messrs.
Stern and Schwarz suppose that the peoples of Europe —
like those of any other continent — would pursue an organized battle, under a centralized command and with a
logistics expending its fuel and munitions, after the fall
of several nuclear missiles and under the threat of "re-
ceiving" still more? And if, by some miracle, such battles
were to continue, would not the blackmail of new thermonuclear damage impose the immediate laying down of
arms, if those arms were ever taken out of the arsenals in
the first place? Can one so easily confront the recollec-
tion of past wars with the use of the new explosive? Why
should the aggressor stop his "escalator" when he has the
weapons of total and definitive victory in his stockpiles?
And why, knowing this, should the militiaman of the attacked nation offer himself to the holocaust? Ordinary
good sense could not accept this illogic. More than any
other armed force, a militia depends on the consent of
those constituting it. Faced with such prospects, how can

we justify a system still more irrational for the defensive side than for the one which, cherishing aggressive intentions, has quite legitimate reasons to believe it will emerge victorious, since it is the side taking the initiative in the use of force? As the European economies prosper, it will be increasingly difficult to gamble on heavy battalions, whether it is a question of regular armies or of militias. Of course, Switzerland is a rich nation, socially and intellectually highly developed, and still bases its security on a militia system. But if it were isolated from its geographical and political context, what would Berne's decision be if it had to choose between the annihilation of several Swiss cities and association with the Eastern nations? Obviously what matters is to ban force by the threat of a penalty which would exceed any advantage the aggressor could derive from war. And under the present conditions, there exists in the West no conventional army — whatever its strength — that can represent such a threat.

The Support of Public Opinion

On almost every page, the reader's attention has been called to the great question of the hour: how associate respect for democratic concepts with the practice of the complex and apparently irrational and dangerous laws of the thermonuclear age? Supplied with information by their administrations, documented by the studies of their experts, some governments are taking account of the security policy they should be pursuing. But few of these are widely understood and in full possession of popular

support; opposition parties have not failed to exploit the
obscurities of the new system of international equilibrium
to complicate their task. Gambling on public ignorance,
it is easy for the opposition to give the appearance of good
sense and realism.

At the end of June 1960, the National Executive Committee of the British Labor Party published a manifesto on
its policy with regard to security. Aside from the fact that
this text reverted to the initial Labor position on the
British dissuasion weapon, it abounded in contradictions.
On the one hand, it implicitly admitted that Great Britain's chief danger lay in the use of the nuclear explosive,
but it forbade possession of the nuclear weapon by West
Germany, which came down to saying that the United
States (and Great Britain) should risk their own existence to guarantee the independence and integrity of a
Germany forbidden to defend herself. The Laborites also
demanded that the West abandon the initiative in using
the H-bomb. This was to invite a surprise attack of thermonuclear aggression. But above all, facing numerically
superior conventional forces, the West was to accept its
defeat rather than use the arsenal it possessed. Lastly,
such a position neutralized the salutary threat constituted
by the "escalator," the rise in the scale of destructive
power culminating in mutual annihilation. Without being aware of it, the Labor Party was undermining the very
foundations of the new form of peace within which, willy-
nilly, we all must live.

The Executive Committee also announced that it was
opposed to the installation of Thor launching sites on
British soil. It demanded that America guarantee the
security of the United Kingdom by accepting the risk of

destruction in its behalf, but could not admit that such a risk be shared, that Great Britain cooperate in her own defense and, to a certain degree, in that of the United States. Despite the illogic and the childish egoism it implies, such a defense policy certainly expressed the opinion of a large share of the British electoral body. Little more would be necessary for this unlikely defense conception to represent the views of a powerful party, an important element of the political life of a great nation, one celebrated, moreover, for the effectiveness of its democratic institutions.

The Atlantic Pact suffers from this divorce between popular judgment and the conceptions technology imposes on military commands and on certain governments. One reason is that when the NATO Pact was signed, technological and strategic conditions were different. It appeared less dangerous than today to show one's teeth and pursue a policy of thermonuclear dissuasion. And as a matter of fact, nothing has fundamentally changed. But how make this understood?

Such, apparently are the profound alterations which have occurred in ten years in the relation of Eastern forces to those of the West: the American territory can be reached by the Soviet missiles; the cost of modern weapons has continued to rise, while their scale has widened daily; the U.S.S.R. has obliged the U.S.A. to enter an exacting scientific and technological race; the underdeveloped nations have noisily taken their place in international life; the race for a higher standard of living has been entered by all nations, and the wealthiest are not the last to wish to accelerate the pace; lastly, technocracy has become an institution. Necessary and effective, it is nonetheless separated from the public opinion it must educate and win to its views. What measures, what texts could resist such upheavals?

As far as the security of Europe is concerned, the many reasons which have radically altered the conditions of its defense — and, as a matter of fact, the means of the political status quo — can be articulated around two major causes.

The first is, of course, the vulnerability of United States territory to attacks which can henceforth be launched against it by a nation the size of the U.S.S.R. or tomorrow's China. Naturally the policy of dissuasion will not thereby be invalidated. It will only be increasingly limited to the defense of absolutely vital stakes and particularly to protecting the nation which possesses such means. Will it retain any credibility if it is used to guarantee a third nation? Will this likelihood of a thermonuclear reaction for the defense of a group of nations — the strategic basis of NATO — endure?

The widening of the scale of hostilities with which the communist world threatens the West is the second of the great upheavals that have occurred since 1950. Mustering considerable intellectual and material means, the West must now confront many other ordeals than the military conquest feared at the time of the signing of the NATO treaty. Of course, the notion — widely held at the time — as to the charge of the Soviet divisions toward the shores of the Atlantic cannot be completely dismissed, but now many other dangers accompany this latter one. When the West grows aware of the diversity of forms which the general encirclement of the positions it still occupies is now assuming, it must realize that, in the military realm, technology has advanced at such a rate, and the panoply it must possess has become so enormous, so complex and so costly, that vast resources must be devoted to it. The West must enter the "invention race" and win it, emerging victorious in almost the entire range of technology, or else lose everything. Aside from the United States, no nation, even by combining its resources with those of other nations, either by integration or association, can keep up with either of the two Great Powers. It appears that the West — even including the United States — is close to reaching the limit in purely military areas, whereas nothing — or almost nothing — has been done to gain victories in other areas that are just as important. Glutted with spiritual and material wealth, the West uses its resources so badly that it cannot make available the means necessary to hold all the battlements that are under attack.

Do cures for these difficulties exist? In the particular case of the defense of Western Europe, analysis suggests a group of remedies to NATO's two weaknesses, the credibility of a nuclear reaction in behalf of a third nation, and the cost and complexity of modern weapons.

The first of the objections to the present *modus vivendi* — and the more serious one — refers to the credibility of a dissuasion policy pursued for the sake of nations other than the one which possesses the means and accepts the risks of action. Of course, the aggressor, too, would run equivalent risks and, by taking the initiative of provocation, would have to play his game of Russian roulette first. But there could be many situations in which the disproportion between the risk and the stake would be so great that a reaction would be highly unlikely. The dangers of the policy of dissuasion can be so manifestly excessive in relation to the value of the stake they are intended to defend that the possibility of a reprisal would be slight and, consequently, the risk ignoring it could readily be taken.

There exist at least two ways of dealing with this danger. One consists in deploying, on the territory of the nation being guaranteed, the forces of the guaranteeing power. In Europe, American school children would play this role just as well as armored divisions, since it is a question of obliging the guaranteeing nation, by a physical presence, to react as it would if threatened directly. But such solutions are obviously neither absolute nor permanent. They have their limitations, which can derive from either one or the other of the governments involved.

The other formula consists in practicing, on the national level, the policy of dissuasion hitherto adopted by the United States for its own defense and for that of its allies in the NATO framework. This method would increase the credibility of a reaction to threat of an attack, for the aggressor would then have to gamble on the national reflex of a people whose very existence was threatened. And it is obviously easier to prepare a quasi-automatic reprisal against aggression on the national level than on the collective level, where each party fears to take part unavailingly in excessive dangers. Because it could be made proportional to the *casus belli,* a punitive reprisal would appear more plausible to the assailant taking the initiative. The community of allied nations would not have to accept *en bloc,* and perhaps for the sake of only one among them, an exorbitant sacrifice which would mean general annihilation. It is toward the generalization of dissuasion on the national level that the world is tending. When scientific and financial resources give out, systems of alliance, with transfer of new weapons placed under a certain control, proliferate.

Distributing the weapons necessary to an effective dissuasion policy can create useless risks. These weapons would therefore be placed under a double check. Hence a dangerous dissemination of nuclear armament would be avoided and a system of dissuasion established that would be national in its use and also collective for the mustering of the necessary means, since it would be based on collective resources for study, experiment, manufacture, and control of these weapons, and on national interest, even national egoism, for their possible use. The formula would conciliate both the imperative of a credible dissuasion and the necessity of sharing the free world's resources for study and manufacture of the weapons necessary to its defense.

In the NATO framework, the dissemination of the ballistic and nuclear weapons necessary to a dissuasion policy on the national level could be considered, as it has been sketched above, in the hypothesis of a bilateral agreement between America and France. The weapons necessary to national dissuasion could be entrusted by the United States to certain allied governments or to friendly regional groups constituted by nations close enough to — and sufficiently dependent on — each other to accept union in the face of danger. The power of this armament, its numerical importance, the "quantity of destruction" it represents would be proportional to the value the potential aggressor is estimated to set upon the nation or nations it wished to attack. These weapons would be placed under a double check; the United States, on one side, and the ally — or group of allies — on the other, would sign an agreement defining their possible conditions of use. This agreement would specify that, if certain danger criteria were fulfilled by the adversary's attitude, Washington would relinquish its check and transfer to its ally the "key" which its representatives held, thereby agreeing to transform an arsenal placed under a double check into the instrument of a purely national defense. And the general terms of such an agreement would be made public. But in order to leave both parties a margin of action, and to create an additional risk for the aggressor, it would be understood that there were other danger criteria than those defined by the agreement.

In Western Europe, this formula cannot be substituted for the other, the one which has proved its worth up to now. It can only be added to it. The NATO Alliance would thereby gain in being better adapted to the new conditions and by gambling on both a collective system and the greater credibility of the national reflex. Besides, resistance to aggression would be organized in depth, consisting of several successive detention lines.

The first of these is formed by the allied conventional forces deployed, according to the formula, as far to the east as possible, and constituted by the array of national contributions and the integration of their command organisms. The units of this "shield" — as it has been called — are gradually to be equipped with small- and medium-caliber atomic charges carried by "vectors" — planes or missiles — with a limited or medium range. These so-called "tactical" atomic charges, aside from the fact that they offset the adversary's numerical superiority, suggest the dreaded "escalator" process and consequently contribute decisively to dissuasion. They form, behind the first, a second line of resistance. The adversary knows that in penetrating it, he would have to run the risk of switching from the system of conventional destruction to the atomic system, to cross the nuclear threshold and consequently enter the "spiral of disaster."

These two lines of resistance, which gain in power according to the degree that they are intermeshed, would depend on the system of collective defense, the tactical atomic weapons being furnished by Washington to its own contingents and, under check, to those of certain allied nations. But the concept of the collective shield plays its part only in so far as there exists a complete identity of outlook among the allied governments. If one of them grew frightened or if it decided that since its own nation was not being directly threatened it would be running an excessive risk, this double line of resistance would be singularly weakened. But if in the third position, after overcoming the first two obstacles, the adversary were obliged to confront the full pressure of the threat of a national reaction, the latter being carried out by weapons placed under a double check, he would have to run a new risk, the likelihood of national resistance then being all the greater, since there would be no ambiguity as to the nature of the threat hanging over the country attacked. The addition of national potentialities to the collective dissuasion policy would actually form a third zone of resistance to aggression. And this zone would be all the firmer and more effective the more exact, serious, and even

— geographically — the more limited the threat. As for the other threats, it would be the job of the first two lines of resistance to "discourage" them.

Still farther behind these lines, across the Atlantic, the possible intervention of the Strategic Air Command in behalf of Western Europe constitutes the fourth of the possible reactions. Decisive because of the extent of the destruction it could mobilize, such intervention appears less credible as the months pass, at least if one takes into account the development of the techniques of offensive weapons and the progress of their antidotes, the anti-missile missiles. This is only a temporary situation, and tomorrow a new technological revolution could change everything. Today, what counts in the present case is that the unlikelihood of use is partially offset by the decisive, absolute, definitive character of such a force of annihilation. So that, merely because it exists, the Strategic Air Command remains one of the elements of dissuasion, even to the advantage of the weakest allies of the United States.

Lastly, as the *ultima ratio,* the "Fortress America" — impregnable and invincible — crowns the structure of Western defense. Who would run the risks inherent in the successive penetration of these defense lines if, having avoided all the pebbles on the road to world hegemony, he would then have to overcome the rock which forbids access to it? What road is so dangerous as one strewn with such obstacles, at times combined with each other or else releasing an all-out avalanche? Especially if one knew, even before confronting these dangers, that the road were ultimately blocked by an immovable boulder?

This reorganization of the Western defense system

would alter neither the spirit nor the letter of the NATO Treaty. Taking technological and strategic development into account, it would add a complementary line of defense to the existing arrangements. Hence the declining credibility of massive nuclear retaliation would be offset and the Allies' uncertain cohesion under the adversary's efforts to divide them would be rendered less dangerous.

The second of the great difficulties the free world confronts today remains to be surmounted: the tremendous increase of the obligations imposed upon it on every side by the diversity of the threats which weigh upon it, by its awareness of new problems like those so harshly imposed by the underdeveloped nations, and also by the considerable widening of the scale of armament techniques which must figure in its panoply. Can it diminish the share absorbed by study and manufacture of these weapons without thereby putting itself in a position of inferiority? Can the West, on the ramparts of this fortress that is surrounded on all sides, hold the same battlements and, economizing a share of the resources they require, hold others now directly under attack?

In the case of the defense of Western Europe, and more generally of the Atlantic Community, the reply can be made affirmatively.

For men of this generation, the term strategy is still defined by the dictionary as "the art of preparing a campaign and of directing an army against decisive points." To strategy we do not yet attribute other virtues than those involving the study and conduct of campaign operations, the ingenious application of the celebrated principles of war to the maneuvering and confrontation of armed forces. It is in this sense that Frederick the Great and Bonaparte were great strategists. And it is in this sense that Clausewitz and Jomini understood the term. For centuries there has not been any other strategy, in the military sense of the term, than that of war operations.

Yet a new form of strategy was born with the wars of the twentieth century. It will here be called the "strategy of means." It includes logistics, but considerably exceeds the latter, since it covers both the study and the manufacture of weapons, their movement, their establishment, their "posture," and also their maintenance. When, in 1944, General Eisenhower launched the Allied invasion of Europe, he was much more a good administrator of a solid and powerful "strategy of means" than a general or a strategist in the classical sense of the word. The power of the combat means mustered under his orders might have been able, to a certain degree at least, to compensate for any tactical faults. Because a certain number of thousands of tons of fuel and munitions had been accumulated where they were needed, because in a period of maximum effort the Allied planes were capable of making more than ten thousand sorties a day, and because the Anglo-American fleet could safely carry across the Channel hundreds of thousands of men, armed and supplied, the result of the battles was never for a moment in doubt. Badly fought, these battles would have slowed down the Allied victory. Masterfully waged, they would have advanced its ultimate occurrence. But the match was won. The Allied strategy of means had triumphed over the strategy of means of the Third Reich.

Five years later, however, either the lesson had already been forgotten or else had not yet been understood. When it was a question, among the Western governments, of reaching an agreement as to a valid defensive system for the atomic age, it was the strategy of operations that was adopted, and to it alone everything was sacrificed. The general staffs were to become interallied and, if necessary, to conduct operations with the aid of troops that would be as integrated as possible. War plans were to be established in common and executed together. In other words, these excellent arrangements indicated that certain lessons of the Second World War were being taken into account.

But at the same time, NATO left to each nation in isolation the responsibility of constituting, training, arming, and supplying the forces that would form its contribution to collective defense. According to NATO's military terminology, "logistics remained national." And not only was logistics — that is, the movement of weapons and their replacement — the concern of each government, but also the conception of armament plans, study, research, development, tests, and the manufacture and improvement of matériel. In practical terms, if the "strategy of operations" was shared, the "strategy of means" remained a national privilege.

In the thermonuclear age, it is a question of preventing war rather than waging it. A healthy and powerful strategy of means can achieve such a result. The planning of campaigns which would lead in a few hours to general chaos is of much less importance than the construction and establishment of weapons capable of outlawing force. Why should thousands of military specialists draw up plans of operations which everyone knows can never be executed? But if priority is given to mustering the means of dissuasion, how can the corresponding enormous resources be accumulated at the national level?

This kind of monopoly granted to the strategy of operations, valid as long as the West alone possessed the weapons of thermonuclear annihilation, now risks running counter to the goal desired. In the NATO framework, the strategy of operations would culminate in a collectively waged struggle, whereas with each nation now calculating its chances of escaping total destruction, there is a diminishing possibility that collective risks would be willingly taken.

The defensive system to which Europe has hitherto owed its safety therefore reveals two great weaknesses: (1) if it covered the threat of general warfare and consequently rendered it unlikely, it would have difficulty resisting the aggressor's limited assaults against an isolated member nation; (2) it has not been able to provide a rational solution to the nevertheless crucial problem of the "strategy of means."

In short, the conditions of the NATO Treaty's functioning must be reversed — that is, the intellectual and material resources which the nations can devote to security must be integrated in order, first, to create and maintain, under better conditions, the arsenal of the strategy of means, whether collective or national; and, second, in order to shift from the collective to the individual plan in carrying out the policy of dissuasion or, at least, in order to add the advantages of the "national reflex" to the collective reactions and thereby compensate, by the former's potentialities, for the latter's limitations.

In practical terms, it will be necessary to transform into a collective organization what is national — that is, muster the means essential to the struggle — and, on the contrary, to shift from the collective to the national level the possible use of the arsenal thus constituted. The organization of collective defense would therefore be more heavily burdened with the financing of the armament plans, with their execution, and also with the distribution to the member nations of the weapons thus manufactured than with their massive utilization — save, of course, in the event of a general conflict.

Many other alterations could still be made in the existing defensive system. In political terms, the problem ten years ago was to create a unit extending from North Cape to Turkey. In military terms, on the other hand, a regional mosaic more or less adapted to the characteristics of the possible theater of operations — North, Central, and Southern — has become necessary. It constitutes today the articulation of the NATO command and armed forces.

The new conditions under which the East-West confrontation is developing lead us to suppose that, politically too, a certain regional organization, conceived in the framework of the NATO Pact as it exists today, would have its advantages. Generalized warfare, like the communist "nibbling," is to be forestalled rather than endured. It is consequently the political strategy which is important, the "posture" of the nations facing the trial by force as much as — and even more than — the "posture" of the armed forces under enemy attack.

The accumulated experience of these last years — and their logic alone — indicates that it will be increasingly difficult to ask governments geographically remote from each other and with various vital interests to combine in order to take in common risks which are henceforth considerable. Regional division will have at least the advantage of greatly reducing these risks. Aside from the fact that it creates a thousand close material ties between nations, geographical proximity gives them, in the face of danger, the feeling of being in the same boat.

Pivotal point of the Western defensive system, the United States would be a member of each of these regional groups. Whether it was the one including the Scandinavian groups and Great Britain, for instance, or the one that would associate, still more closely, the nations of "Center Europe," America would be present, as she is, moreover, in all the regional pacts she has hitherto concluded and which, juxtaposed, seal the Western defensive perimeter. It is in the framework of these regional groupings that the modalities of the policy of national — or regional — dissuasion and the transfer of arms under double check would be negotiated.

A guaranteeing power until the moment she chose to gamble on the "national reflex" of the threatened power, the regional system would limit the risks America would be asked to run. By pursuing her dissuasion policy for the sake of the Atlantic collectivity as a whole, as for the benefit of each of its members, it would be easier to find a just proportion between the form aggression might take and the extent of the retaliation necessary. Consequently the American guarantee would appear more credible: it would be sufficiently feared so that an aggressor would not dare provoke its realization.

To review the solutions which the conditions of the new weapons' use suggest leads to the following proposals: in Europe, a security force based on the combination of conventional forces — each a contribution to the system of common defense — and of strategic nuclear forces belonging, individually or in common (double check), to the chief guaranteeing powers; outside Europe, far from the sanctuary protected at any — or almost any — cost, nothing is as valuable as the presence of guaranteeing forces, but we know that such presence is not always desirable to the autochthonous power. The adversary almost always manages to create the initial conditions, consequently the West must have the determination and the capacity to shift its forces of "presence" almost instantaneously, materializing the determination to resist and, consequently, enforcing the dangers of the "escalator." But most important of all is a "good diplomacy" which forestalls both subversion and the *coup d'état.*

By gradually adding their own atomic arsenals to those of the United States, Great Britain, and the U.S.S.R., other nations will also be capable of discouraging any impulse of aggression toward themselves. They will in part lighten the responsibilities which the guaranteeing powers can moreover no longer assume save in an uncertain fashion.

If this must be the direction of the development, and if the movement is as irreversible as the one which culminated in the generalization of firearms, it would be better for the Western nations to reach an understanding — either at the Atlantic level, or at the European one — in order to create this common arsenal and to give it its true significance, with regard to generalized dissuasion, by distributing its weapons among the cooperating states.

Few subscribe to this policy. Until it is adopted or a substitute for it is found, it is obvious that the threat of

massive reprisal wielded by the guaranteeing states in behalf of the others is losing its power. Though the thermonuclear ballistic missile is still in its embryonic state, its
omnipotence finds fewer and fewer stakes corresponding
to its measure. Without this weapon, the rupture of
equilibrium would be brutal; yet it is not enough to create
stability in itself, which is what it is censured for. Re-
calling — unconsciously — the celebrated syllogism of the
"rare horse," a general wrote that the thermonuclear
weapons were so powerful that they removed any prospect of world conflict, that it was therefore highly unlikely that such weapons would ever be used and that consequently they should be discarded. Despite its absurdity,
this reasoning is frequently invoked. As a matter of fact,
so long as the United States alone possessed a powerful
Strategic Air Command, it held — without risk and
cheaply enough — the chief bastions. Today, this force
holds only one battlement. The others remain to be defended.[1] When, from the tribunal of the French Senate,
Monsieur Soustelle declared that "the creation of an au-
tonomous thermonuclear force is among the concerns of
the French government," the Minister doubtless meant

[1] This is more or less the theme of General Maxwell Taylor's second work.
The former chief of the American Army's general staff asks his government
to substitute for the notion of "massive reprisal" a strategy of "modified
response" — i.e., that the classical arms race be resumed, offsetting the advantages the adversary might derive from numerical superiority by better
(?) techniques. This is also the position taken by certain British experts,
as echoed by *The Economist* when it opposed the notions of Mr. Duncan
Sandys concerning the defense of the British Isles by the threat of a
Bomber Command reprisal. In short, so long as there were no risks in basing security on dissuasion, everyone subscribed to this policy. As soon as
it seems to call for boldness, everyone reverts to notions that had been rejected some years ago and that based defense on manpower rather than on
machines and explosives. But by thus humanizing it, war again becomes
possible.

Leninist-Stalinist concept of capitalist encirclement, to accentuate the state of tension — in short to justify an exceptional regime by the very extent of the threats which always weigh on the socialist world in general and on the U.S.S.R. in particular.

Consequently, in its great naïveté, the free world imagined itself balked of a peace which one side would supposedly have facilitated by suddenly — and unilaterally — limiting its ambitions, and the other would have accepted because it gave assurance of maintaining, at last, a hitherto threatened status quo. After May 1960, these illusions were dissipated and the erosion of one world by the other resumed.

Today, however, the material means capable of imposing the abandonment of force, of neutralizing numerical superiority and of obliging the majority to respect the minority — the inverse is also true — exist. Because the risks inherent in the use of the atomic explosive are considerable, and because the world knows it — in part thanks to Soviet propaganda — the state of peace among nations can be much more stable than formerly, when the value of forces "in presence" was estimated and this estimate was made with a heart all the lighter in that the penalty was never total and one could always gamble on the "fortunes of war." Tomorrow, the penalty will be instantaneous and invariably fail to correspond to the very stake of the dispute.

Now we must understand, and make ourselves understood. We must raze the old structure of conventional confrontations, sweep away the remains of a historical conception without analogies with the present, and seize in all its implications the new logic of the atom. Despite its

apparent subtleties, the democracies must popularize the
rules of this logic in order to achieve unanimity in its regard. Whether we want to or not, we have entered the
nuclear cycle. And it happens that it is at our service. Or
rather, it will serve us provided we understand its laws.